MW01073661

NO OPPORTUNITY WASTED

THE ART OF EXECUTION

JOSEPH W. WALKER III

Published in Nashville, Tennessee, by Heritage Publishing

Library of Congress Cataloging-in-Publishing Data

ISBN 978-0-9974318-5-8

CONTENTS

INTRODUCTION

When I released *Reset*, I had no idea how many lives would be impacted by the strategies within the book. That book was birthed out of my passion to see people move beyond their personal setbacks and disappointments and pursue God's best for their lives. When we reset, we make an intentional decision to engage in a journey toward the redevelopment and redefining of who we are after what could be *life-altering* events. This process is not for the faint of heart, rather it is for the courageous few who have concluded that a reset will bring out their best. As with *Reset*, this book is also birthed out of a passion to see people succeed in every area of their lives.

I've been leading a thriving congregation for 25 years and training leaders for over 20. I've seen great ideas put on the table but die "in committee," because there was no strategy to move them forward. Vision is a powerful thing. If you are blessed to have it, you know that it can consume you. How many meetings have you sat in where great ideas were put forth but never came to fruition? There is no shortage of ideas, philosophical debate, or highly opinionated people.

I spent three intense years in divinity school pursuing a master's degree; but when I finished, I realized I was theoretically proficient but illiterate in terms of practical application. I had studied systematic theology, soteriology, epistemology, and even pneumatology. Yet, I had never baptized a person until I was a pastor. I had never served Communion until I served a church as a pastor. Talk about a learning curve.

From the ivory halls of the academy to corporate boardrooms, even to the hallowed pews of our places of worship, we are inundated with information on what should be done, but few of us are actually given the practical strategies about how to do it. I'm reminded of the apostle Paul's internal struggle that he shares regarding "what" and "how." "For I know that in me (that is, in my flesh,) dwelleth no good thing: for to will is present with me; but how to perform that which is good I find not" (Romans 7:18, KJV). Paul's struggle for the "how" is a universal struggle. The world needs not only your "what" but your "how"—your know-how. Your vision means nothing if it is out in some theoretical space but never comes down to the real world of practicality and implementation.

One of the things I've observed among some incredibly successful people is the guarding of their "how." Many of them willingly share what they have accomplished but only give cursory remarks concerning how they actually did it. To be fair, there are legitimate reasons for why they do this. Some of them fear the erroneous replication of their brand. Others fear that someone will take their strategies and move toward implementation while totally dismissing the sweat equity. This guarded approach is completely understandable and gives me even greater excitement about this book. Everything that works for one organization may not work for yours, but it is essential that you have a comprehensive understanding of what it takes to execute vision.

Now that you have reset your life, it's time to move toward the manifestation of your new and approved destiny. This is not a sprint; it's a marathon. There will be key lessons you must learn along the way. This book is about the hard work necessary in bringing theory into concrete reality, praxis—what ought to be to become what can be. It's about measurable results, but mostly it's about not wasting opportunities and making the most of the opportunities you take on.

I am prayerful that anyone serious about producing results will employ the strategies in the pages of this book. They have been tested and proven effective over the many years I have been a leader. I may have started with only trial and error, but you don't have to. I'm excited about your NOW and how the art of execution will release the vision within you.

1

YOU WERE BORN TO SOLVE A PROBLEM

One of the most common questions I hear from people is, "What is my purpose?" There have been numerous books written on this subject. Purpose is critical if you are going to make any significant contribution in life. Knowing why you are here and God's will for your life should be at the top of your list of priorities. Knowing that will position you not to waste opportunities that will propel your God-given vision.

When you think about purpose, it's important to know that purpose is in the mind of the Maker. When a builder builds a structure, he or she has to take into account all the things necessary for the building to align with its original purpose. When Detroit begins a new car concept, the design is a result of the purpose and vision of the design team. This is why minivans are designed differently than sports cars. Their purpose is different.

Conversely, God created you with a purpose in mind. Everything about us was designed with the purpose in mind. Our personality, strengths, and even our passions all point toward the purpose for which we were placed on this planet. Don't waste them.

Imagine there is a problem. That's not a hard thing to do with so many choices. Each one of the problems has an answer here on Earth. Hopefully, someone somewhere is operating with purpose to help bring resolution. Whether it is a community leader or a researcher, problems are being solved because problem-solvers are walking in purpose. On the flip side, someone could be dead and buried who had the cure to cancer, but the problem was never addressed because they did not fulfil their purpose on Earth.

God created us with a purpose in mind.

See yourself as a catalyst for change so that the purposes of God can be manifested in your life. The late Dr. Myles Munroe used to say that we "must die empty." It is a tragedy when we take the purposes God has placed within us to the grave. We must make sure our lives fulfill our God-given assignment, so that everything in us is released on Earth. This is why Paul says in Philippians 1:6 (KJV), "Being confident of this very thing, that he which hath begun a good work in you will perform it until the day of Jesus Christ."

Ask yourself, *What problem was I created to solve?* It is essential that you discover the purpose you were placed on Earth to fulfill because your purpose is the solution to someone's problem. Albert Einstein once stated, "We cannot solve our problems with the same level of thinking that created them." Elevating your thinking will help you tap into the purpose you were designed to accomplish. A change in mindset is necessary to get you off the ground level of your situation and move you to a higher level, leading to a stratosphere of solutions. Mountaintop thinking will help you solve a mountain of problems in life.

Your purpose is the solution to someone else's problem.

People ask me, "How did you know you were called to be in ministry?" From an early age I knew I was different. My grandmother would share with my mother that I was a unique child. When I was in elementary school, my level of energy made it difficult for teachers to deal with me. I was often sent to the principal's office or reprimanded by teachers because I wouldn't sit down or seemingly wasn't paying attention. I learned early on that when people don't know what do to with you, it's easier to put you in a particular classification or category in order to define you. Often, these characterizations have lasting impacts on children.

I was blessed to have parents who were engaged in my life and who made frequent visits to the school. As a result, I was not put into a category that stigmatized me for the rest of my life. They discovered I was bored and actually gifted. Consequently, they introduced me to music, and all that energy was focused on playing the drums.

It would be the drums that helped me gain a scholarship to Southern University Baton Rouge. I was privileged to march in the band, which helped discipline me as a man and put me on a path toward my ultimate purpose. It was at Southern University while majoring in English that I became determined to go to law school. I had several siblings who had become successful attorneys and judges, and I wanted to be the "Black Matlock." I was certain this would be my purpose. I loved to read and write. I had tons of energy and enjoyed making my case in healthy debates. There was no doubt in anybody's mind that this nerdy kid in the marching band was poised to be an attorney one day.

Mountaintop thinking will help you solve a mountain of life's problems.

Let me say a word about ambition. Webster defines it as "a strong desire to achieve something, typically requiring determination and hard work." Ambition is not a bad thing, but it can often blind us to our purpose. When you are ambitious, you are driven with determination. The emotional investment and sweat equity you put into what you are after is hard to negate. It can create a level of anxiety when you are told to abandon your plans for something that wasn't on your radar.

I was locked in on my dream. I had wanted this since I was a child. I was walking in the shadow of my siblings. Nothing anyone could have told me could have made me believe it wasn't going to happen. I was all in.

All of that would change one day as I was standing under my fraternity tree with a crowd of frat brothers. That moment was as surreal then as it is as I write it now. Although I was in the midst of a noisy crowd, everything went mute. It wasn't a natural event; it was a spiritual one. I saw people talking, but everything seemed to be tuned out. There was a still, small voice in my spirit summoning me to a call higher than my lifelong desire to be an attorney. It was a call to serve God's people in ministry, but nothing in me at the moment wanted to accept it.

One of the truest signs you are being called into purpose is that your flesh will resist it. I asked the Lord if He didn't mean to call another Joseph? As ridiculous as it sounds, I felt like God had made a mistake and called the wrong person. Moses resisted his call because of his age and speech impediment. Joshua resisted his call because he felt he was too young. Jonah ran as far as he could prior to yielding to the call on his life. I ran literally and figuratively.

An interesting thing occurred when I resisted the call. I could not sleep. I could not focus. I could barely eat. I couldn't figure out what was going on, until I realized things would not be the same until I said yes. Like Jonah wrestling in the belly of the fish, he was not delivered until he said yes. God was looking for my yes. My mother used to say, "You can run but you can't hide from God." I would discover this in a personal and profound way.

Perhaps you are reading this and you are in the midst of being called into purpose. Please understand that an "all right then" response is fundamentally different than a yes. When we are willing to walk in our purpose, we must be willing to completely yield. But if we go only with an "all right then" response, we go reluctantly and often keep our foot in the door so that other options remain open. Perhaps this is why Jesus says in Matthew 16:24 (NIV), "Whoever wants to be my disciple must deny themselves and take up their cross and follow me." I had to deny my personal will in exchange for His will for my life. Once that happened, I began to understand that what was happening in my life did not start at that moment but had its genesis long before that moment.

Romans 8:28-30 became the biblical foundation for me to understand how purpose came to pass in my life. We often only quote verse 28 and tell people that all things are going to work together for their good. Although this sounds like a good remedy for the challenges we all face, this verse specifically speaks to those who "love God, to them who are the called according to his purpose." If you are not in that category, there are no guarantees that things will ultimately work out for your good. Paul says:

> And we know that all things work together for good to those who love God, to those who are the called according to His purpose. For whom He foreknew, He also predestined to be conformed to the image of His Son, that He might be the firstborn among many brethren. Moreover whom He predestined, these He also called; whom He called, these He also justified; and whom He justified, these He also glorified.
>
> (Romans 8:28-30)

Let's examine this in relationship to the process of being called into purpose.

What does it mean to be foreknown? Imagine prior to your mother meeting your father and your grandmother meeting your grandfather that God had you in mind. Their encounters were not accidents but were part of a divine plan to bring you into being.

Their DNA, pedigree, and personalities would flow through your bloodline to produce the person you are today. You were wired for purpose.

God gave me my father's energy, my mother's compassion, my grandmother's discernment, and my grandfather's wit. All of these attributes would be important in the fulfilment of my purpose. I needed that energy to pastor a church with eight services weekly. I needed that compassion to have a heart for people and service. I needed that discernment to make critical decisions as a leader, and I needed wit to challenge a thriving congregation spiritually and intellectually. All of those traits that came together in me were things that God started long before the day I was born. Essentially, I was born into purpose but didn't quite know it until I was 20 years old.

It was at age 20 that God called me to what was already inside me. That experience under my fraternity tree was a clear call to purpose. It was a call to the thing that had begun before I began. The problem was an earthly problem, and I was called forth to bring resolution to it.

To understand the call, you have to know that you are never called without a destination. A call is never ambiguous. God never calls and then says, "Let me figure out what I want to do with you." A call is specific to purpose. You might ask, "What about Abraham's call to ministry? Wasn't his call ambiguous?" Although Abraham was not given all the details of his assignment, he knew that God was leading him to a land that would be shown to him in God's time. Genesis 12:1-3 records the following message from the Lord to Abraham (Abram),

> Get out of your country, from your family and from your father's house, to a land that I will show you. I will make you a great nation; I will bless you and make your name great; and you shall be a blessing. I will bless those who bless you, and I will curse him who curses you; and in you all the families of the earth shall be blessed.

The Lord did not provide Abraham with all the logistical details, but Abraham was given clear instructions.

1. Get out of your country, from your family, and father's house.
2. I will show you the land where I am sending you.
3. I will make you a great nation, and you will be blessed.
4. And as a result of your pursuit of purpose, all the families who come from your lineage of faith will be blessed.

God never calls us from nothing. He calls us to something.

The totality of the purpose may not be disclosed, but the purpose itself is clear and concise.

Moses was called to liberate God's people from Egyptian bondage. Joshua was called to bring God's people into the Promised Land. The disciples were called to be fishers of men. Paul was called to share the gospel around the world. In each one of these examples, the person called was called while doing something. Moses was keeping sheep, and later he mentored Joshua to serve God's people. Saul (Paul) was using his energy and influence to persecute Christians. I was in school preparing to become an attorney.

God never calls us from nothing. He calls us while we are actively doing something. You cannot expect to be summoned into purpose if you are idle. God calls us from something to a clear something.

> God never chooses perfect people because He has none to choose from.

Another significant point is that when God calls us, He calls us to Him first. He calls us prior to the assignment or purpose. If we attempt to walk in purpose apart from relationship with Him, our motives taint the intent of the purpose. In many cases it becomes about us rather than about the God who calls us.

Jesus says in John 6:38 (NIV), "For I have come down from heaven not to do my will but to do the will of him who sent me." Early in my ministry, I watched great things happen and thought it was about me. I found myself at the altar thanking God for using me in such powerful ways. Though my words were appropriate, God knew I was slipping beyond the threshold of humility. I heard His voice clearer that day than ever before in my life. He said, "You're insignificant to the process. This is for My glory."

I then understood how easily hubris, pride, can rise up in any of us and how essential humility is for our lives. Since that day, I've gotten out of God's way and allowed Him to get all the glory. He is not interested in sharing glory with us. Whatever purposes are manifested in our lives are for His glory, not ours.

The next stage of arriving at purpose is working through your inadequacies. Paul says God "justifies." This word suggests that He gives us an acquittal from our past deeds. When I was called to purpose, I gave God a litany of reasons why I didn't feel qualified to do what He was asking me to do. The weight of the assignments to which we are called are inevitably affected by the counterweights of our short-comings and past failures. So God qualifies us when He calls us. There is nothing about you that He doesn't know.

In 1 Samuel 9, King David summons Mephibosheth to Jerusalem for a blessing. Mephibosheth was the youngest and only surviving grandson of King Saul, and he was a cripple. This text has always encouraged me because it reminds us that God knows we are "crippled" when He calls us. God never chooses perfect people because He has none to choose from. He takes your mess and turns it into a message.

Everybody God calls has a not-so-pleasant past, but He uses it for His glory. You don't have to remind God about your shortcomings. He has factored that in when He called you. He justified you for the assignment. As a matter of fact, your experiences will be instrumental in the fulfilment of your purpose in the earth. The things you've done well and not-so-well will be a point of identification for those who will be impacted by your purpose.

God takes your mess and turns it into a message.

Never allow people to judge and label you. Based on their view, they believe you are incapable of grasping the future God has for you because of your past. However, it has been said, and I agree, that God used Abraham who was old; Elijah who was suicidal; Joseph who was abused; Job who went bankrupt; Moses who had a speech problem; Gideon who was afraid; Samson who was a womanizer; Rahab who was a prostitute; the Samaritan woman who was divorced; and Noah who was a drunkard. We know Jeremiah was young. Jacob was a cheater. David was a murderer.

Jonah ran from God. Naomi was a widow. Peter denied Christ three times. Martha worried about everything. Zacchaeus was small and money-hungry. The disciples fell asleep while praying. And Paul was a Pharisee who persecuted Christians before becoming one. The list goes on.

The beauty of purpose is how God perfectly uses imperfection. I could never preach about setbacks if I had never experienced them myself. Often, it is our own stories that bring credibility and authenticity to our purposes. This is what makes following Jesus Christ so amazing, because He identifies with our weaknesses. Hebrews 4:15 (NIV) says, "For we do not have a high priest who is unable to empathize with our weaknesses, but we have one who has been tempted in every way just as we are—yet He did not sin."

Once we are able to move beyond our inadequacies, we enter into what Paul calls "glorification." Though this has eschatological implications, it also speaks to the levels to which God desires to take us when we completely submit to purpose.

I had it all figured out. I thought law was my path in life. I probably would have made a pretty good attorney and could have done a lot of good, but what I learned early in life is that every good thing is not a God thing. I often remind students to choose a major wisely. It is difficult to chase money through a major and get three years into that major only to discover it's not your purpose. Proverbs 10:22 says, "The blessing of the LORD makes one rich, and He adds no sorrow with it." The word *rich* here is not associated with money. Rather, it's referring to completeness.

It's not that God doesn't want you to have blessings, but they should not add sorrow to your life. Purpose should not come with overwhelming stress, marital discord, parental disconnect, physical neglect, or spiritual abandonment. God assured me that I could reach heights walking in His purpose that were far beyond anything I would have imagined pursuing my own will. There are levels to which God wants to take you that are unimaginable. I would have never imagined when God called me under my fraternity tree as a graduating senior headed to law school that He would have elevated me to the heights He has. It is true what Paul says in 1 Corinthians 2:9: "Eye has not seen, nor ear heard, nor have entered into the heart of man the things which God has prepared for those who love Him."

> When you embrace your purpose, you live in confidence that you were born for this.

It is essential that we realize that we are not elevated in purpose for self-serving reasons. God does it that we might make an impact in the world. Remember, you were born to solve a problem, not to create one. When you are in tune with the will of God for your life, you are able to embrace your purpose and confront the problems you face with the confidence that you were born for this.

SIX STAGES OF PURPOSE

I've often shared the following six stages of purpose to help persons measure where they were in the process of it discovering their purpose.

1. Predestined. This is the reality that God was at work in your life before you were born. Regardless of the circumstances of your birth, you are not an accident. You were born a *world-changer.*

2. Passion. This is what God placed in you that gave you a propensity toward the thing He was calling you to. Passion begins at an early age but is not focused. It's like light. When you focus light, it can become a laser and cut through steel. When passion is focused, it is a result of maturity. As you grow and experience life, you gravitate toward things you are passionate about. This gives you a glimpse of your overall purpose. If you are not passionate about children, you probably are not called to childcare. Your purpose will be consistent with your passion.

3. Purpose. After our passions are clear, our purpose is often revealed by a call from God. Although it may not be what we imagined, our purpose will be an organic part of who we are.

4. Preparation. One of the first things my pastor told me when I was called to preach is that it was a call to preparation. That has remained with me over the years. You will never prepare for something you are not passionate about nor sincerely purposed to do. Jesus spent 30 years preparing for a three-year public ministry. We will never be effective in our purpose if we are not learning best practices and developing our craft.

5. Positioning. Preparation puts us in strategic positions. Doors and opportunities open up for those who are prepared for them. Perhaps you are preparing now and wondering about where you are going to be when you graduate or finish your training. God has assigned a position for you that is consistent with your preparation. I would have never guessed in a million years that a kid from Shreveport, Louisiana, would be in Nashville, Tennessee.

The position was there, just waiting on me to be prepared to walk into it.

I love the game of football. One of the plays most teams run is a timing pattern. This is when the receiver runs down the field 15 yards and cuts across five yards. The defensive back knows the play when he sees it coming, so in an attempt to prevent it from unfolding, he hits the receiver with a legal hit at the line of scrimmage. This hit is designed to throw him off his route.

Whenever you are prepared and are headed toward position, expect a hit from the enemy. Those who have been properly prepared absorb the hit and keep running the route. While the receiver is running his route, his back is to the quarterback. The quarterback is not throwing the ball to a person; he is throwing it to a spot. The ball is in the air. All the receiver has to do is get to that spot. If you prepare yourself and get to the spot where God wants you to be, the blessing is already in the atmosphere and will meet you in that place.

6. Produce. The final thing I share is that when it's all said and done, purpose has to produce fruit. The end game is that purpose makes you highly productive. Your life will produce much fruit. Jesus says in John 15:8, "By this My Father is glorified, that you bear much fruit; so you will be My disciples."

LIVING WITH PURPOSE, ON PURPOSE

It's important to understand alignment. Alignment with God's will for your life keeps things in order. Aligning with God will help you recognize opportunity. If you are not together with God, no other relationship in your life will be together.

Often, people wonder why their personal and business relationships remain frustrated. It's because they are running from their God-given purpose. As a consequence, they are out of order. Matthew 6:33 reminds us to "seek first the kingdom of God . . . and all these things shall be added to you."

If you see a vending machine with an out-of-order sign on it, you don't put money in it. You know that any investment will not yield a return because the machine is out of order. Conversely, God nor people of good will won't invest in you if you are out of order. Be willing to submit to God's will for your life.

Purpose is a powerful thing. Since I've been in purpose, I've never worked another day of my life. Every day I wake up, I go to "purpose." You've got to decide if you are going to go to a job for the rest of your life or if you're going to purpose with purpose, on purpose.

God wants you to be significant.

One of the sure signs you are going to purpose is peace. I've shared with students that getting at peace is not the absence of tension. Rather, it is the revelation of God's presence in your life as you walk in His will. When you walk in purpose, you are not affected by the changing or tumultuous seasons you experience. Your walk in purpose is filled with the contentment that you are fulfilling a purpose much larger than yours. God has chosen you to affect change. The problem you are called to solve is unique. Everything about you is uniquely designed by the Creator to make a significant impact in the world.

We live in a world where people chase success. There is nothing wrong with success, but there is a higher pursuit. That's what I want to share with you. It's called significance. When you are significant, you leave an imprint in the world that lives far beyond you. There are many successful people who died and left no significant impact beyond the scope of their own personal success. When our lives elevate and enhance the lives of others around us, we transcend the limitations of personal success and leave on record our significance.

Steve Jobs, the cofounder of Apple Inc., was incredibly successful, but his contributions made him significant. The way we communicate through technology has been changed forever because of his willingness to walk completely in purpose and solve a problem. Long after his death, the entire world and generations to come will benefit from the products his purpose produced.

It doesn't matter what sector of society you are in, we all have a God-given purpose that is designed to solve an earthly problem. Can you imagine a day when every person walks in purpose? Can you imagine a world where everyone seizes the opportunities they have available to them, where nothing and no one is wasted? Many of the challenges we face could be solved by courageous people who walk in purpose.

QUESTIONS

1. What is your purpose? How did God reveal it to you?
2. What dreams have you had to release so that you could walk in divine purpose?
3. What have you gleaned from your life experiences that could help solve someone else's problems?
4. How can you be a catalyst for change?
5. At what stage are you in the stages of purpose?

2

DON'T MISS THE MOMENT

Now that you have a comprehensive understanding of purpose and how it should manifest in your life, it is critical for you to discern the moments when you can activate your vision. There are countless people who have allowed moments, opportunities, to come and go, because they were either not sensitive to their spiritual surroundings or were victims of analysis paralysis.

One of the things that you must possess is a sense of urgency. Your preparation is for these moments, and you have to be ready when they arrive. Second-guessing yourself robs you of God's best. In this chapter, I want to give you specific strategies on identifying moments so that you don't miss them.

Be ready for your opportunity!

HOW TO IDENTIFY OPPORTUNITIES

Let's examine how to identify moments of opportunity. Every opportunity that presents itself is not sent from God. Remember what we mentioned in the previous chapter: Every good thing is not necessarily a God thing. James 1:17 (NIV) declares, "Every good and perfect gift is from above, coming down from the Father of the heavenly lights, who does not change like shifting shadows." There are three keys to discerning these moments.

1. The first key is knowing that moments come with the right timing. When God sends moments in our lives, He has already factored in where we are in our developmental and maturation process. He would never send something you were not ready to handle. Urgency must be tempered with trusting His timetable. God's moments cannot be scheduled on your watch.

Many of us become frustrated because we think we can determine our "when." God controls our "when." He operates in *kairos* moments that are divinely preset to bring us into blessings and amazing opportunities. Everything God does runs on His divine schedule. If you remain faithful where you are, the moment will find you. You won't have to chase it. It doesn't matter how young or old you are. Abraham and Sarah are classic examples that nothing is impossible with God.

Wait for it. The opportunity will find you.

As you read this book, you might be experiencing some level of anxiety around time. It's difficult watching moments come for others, especially when yours are taking longer than what you expect. You cannot allow yourself to be discouraged. Remembering that God's timing is perfect will help put your wait in perspective.

Part of the wait is determining your preparedness for the opportunity. I often tell people that God doesn't promote because of tenure. He promotes because people pass tests. God will orchestrate a series of tests in your life that will reveal your level of maturity for the opportunities ahead of you. It's during these tests that your character, resilience, and faith are revealed.

Am I ready to handle everything that comes with this opportunity?

We often find ourselves grumbling and questioning why we have to experience particular tests, when we should be thankful that they are positioning us for greater opportunities ahead. This is what Peter shares in 1 Peter 5:10 (ESV): "And after you have suffered a little while, the God of all grace, who has called you to his eternal glory in Christ, will himself restore, confirm, strengthen, and establish you."

The three Hebrews boys were promoted after the fiery furnace test, and Job received double after his ordeal. Some people don't have the tough skin necessary to handle certain opportunities. You can have the skillset but not the maturity to deal with everything that comes with opportunity. For example, there can be highly sensitive matters that you are exposed to in particular opportunities that might shake other people to their foundation if they are not seasoned to deal with such matters.

I've seen incredibly gifted people who could not vacillate between the "living room" and the "kitchen" of opportunities. Things that are public knowledge are usually categorized as "living room" matters, but highly sensitive and private matters are described as "kitchen" talk. When you've been through a series of difficult personal experiences, you become more acclimated to handling all situations.

This is why it is necessary to allow yourself to be developed prior to walking through a door into a situation that you're not prepared to handle. I've seen some awesome people who moved too soon. Ask yourself, *Am I ready to handle everything that comes with this opportunity*? I can assure you that the job description is just the tip of the iceberg.

If you can remind yourself that a delay is not a denial, you will be less inclined to jump ahead of God's timetable for your life. Every opportunity that God has ever allowed me to walk into was preceded by a test. I'm sure as you reflect over your life, you can also see a pattern that confirms how awesome God's timing is.

Everything will be in sync.

As much as we would love to embrace certain opportunities, we have to be honest with ourselves and be okay declining them. One of the things the enemy will do is make you believe that this is your one and only opportunity. It doesn't work that way. If you are ready for what's before you, God will send the right thing at the right time into your life. When you think about how David was chosen, it was a result of God's timing. The entire time he was in the backyard tending sheep. When that moment comes, it will be God's way of declaring, "You're ready."

2. The second thing that confirms to us that the opportunity presented before us is the right one is this: Everything will be in sync. There will be interrelated harmony. When opportunities come, realize that God has factored in everything about you—your family, your finances, and your future. Though new opportunities are designed to stretch us beyond our comfort zones, they will not bring disharmony and destruction to the things God has blessed us with. The best way to explain this is to say it will be a logical transition. It won't be forced. If you find yourself struggling to make sense out of it or explain it, it probably is not the opportunity for you.

The beauty of harmony in music is that you can add as many notes as you want to a chord as long as they don't compromise the chord structure. Harmony is not affected by the volume of keys you touch; it is impacted by the wrong keys you touch.

Disharmony in our lives cannot be ignored. When something doesn't fit our lifestyle, it should be apparent. Parents with small children may be presented an opportunity that involves incredible pay but requires them to travel abroad six months out of the year. Though it's a great opportunity, it may not be congruent with their lifestyle. Likewise, a single person with no family might consider this a great opportunity to explore the world without conflicting with significant relationships. This is why you cannot jump at every opportunity without first examining the impact it will have on every aspect of your life. It comes down to priorities.

What I've learned to do is prioritize life in such a way that opportunities are vetted against what's important to me and my family. There is no shortage of opportunities that are presented to me, but I've made a decision to put family first. There is no amount of money that can change that.

When you find yourself compromising your priorities to embrace opportunities, it can become a slippery slope. There was a time when I embraced opportunities at face value without examining their impact on the other areas of my life. This was so unhealthy that I became unnecessarily stressed and frustrated just trying to manage it all. I found myself rescheduling date nights with my wife and telling my daughter I would attend her functions "next time." I knew something had to be done if I was going to bring things into order.

Once you start accepting everything that comes your way, the expectation is that you will just magically make it happen, even if you don't have the personal bandwidth available. One of the most profound lessons I learned—and I pray you learn as well—is that no is an answer. Just because you say no does not diminish the significance of the opportunity, nor should it be viewed as disrespectful to the person who extended it. Guard what's important to assure there is harmony in your life.

One of the strategic and intentional things I do is share with my staff and those around me what's important. By doing this, it gives them a greater sensitivity to the things I'm willing to engage. My professional calendar is set after my personal calendar is in place. Everything submits to my family, thereby creating harmony in my life. When you are juggling a lot, be prayerful and selective about the things you add to your plate because it all has to make sense. Don't sacrifice your personal happiness on the altar of opportunity.

My wife shared with me something one of her mentors shared with her. He was an accomplished person in his field. He had written many books and articles. He had traveled the world and was recognized as one of the top persons in his profession. During their conversation, he shared with her how he lost his wife to divorce and that his children were estranged from him because he was never in their lives. As he reflected upon it all, he felt he could have written one less book, taken one less engagement, or did one less lecture; and his life could have possibly been different. Accolades and accomplishment are important, but they mean nothing if the cost is too high.

The opportunity will not just be about you.

3. The third confirmation that the opportunity is for you is this: The moment will not just be about you. When opportunities come from God, they are sent to bless more than you. There is nothing wrong with having a personal vision about where you want your life to go and what you would like to achieve, but the right opportunities are not exclusive to you. They are designed to elevate those in your sphere of influence. Be willing to take more than you with you when you walk through the door.

Sometimes we are so blinded by our own ambition that we fail to see the larger picture. God sends opportunities and moments into your life because He can trust you to be a good steward with them. This is why Matthew 22:14 (ESV) says, "For many are called, but few are chosen." When it's your moment, you are chosen to walk into knowing that the lives of others are going to be positively affected.

God got Joseph through the door in Egypt and to the table with the king. Though it was a tumultuous journey filled with deception, hatred, accusation, imprisonment, and vindication, all of it was part of God's divine plan for a moment. When Joseph realized that his moment and opportunity were not just about him, his words in Genesis 50:20 put it all in perspective. The NIV version says: "You intended to harm me, but God intended it for good to accomplish what is now being done, the saving of many lives."

Your moment has far-reaching implications. This is why you must not take adversity personally. It's larger than you. When there is destiny on your life, the devil can't take it from you. What he will do is try to make it so rough that you will surrender it yourself. Before you quit, remember that he is not after you. Rather, he's after all the lives that will be impacted by you embracing this opportunity and moment. If I were thinking about me only, I would have gone back to Shreveport, Louisiana, and done what I wanted to do.

I often think back to the moment when I was called to lead the Mount Zion Baptist Church. All three of these strategies were at work. The timing, harmony, and selfless assignment impacted the lives of people on an unimaginable scale. What I have come to discover is that the providential hand of God was at work in my life, so when the moment arrived, it was clear it was God. If I had not embraced the moment, I would have forfeited all the things God wanted to do in and through my life.

I must admit that when I embraced the moment, things didn't appear as I thought they should. I thought Mount Zion was a stepping stone to something greater up the road. This is why the Bible reminds us in Zechariah 4:10 (NLT), "Do not despise these small beginnings." You can miss your blessing minimizing your moment.

God may not reveal the total picture to you, but rest assured He is still painting on the canvas of your future. This is why it was important to me to give it my all early on in my moment. I worked extremely hard making certain that I gave the assignment everything God had put into me. I preached to hundreds like I was preaching to thousands. Matthew 25:23 (NIV) says, "His master replied, 'Well done, good and faithful servant! You have been faithful with a few things; I will put you in charge of many things.' " When the moment comes, put in the work regardless of what it looks like to you now.

When your moment comes, walk into it with confidence and certainty. Embrace it knowing that God thought enough of you to give you this chance. Go all in! Don't *half-step* waiting on it to look like what you envisioned. Trust God and know that He doesn't waste moments. Everything that has happened in your life was interrelated and necessary for this moment to emerge for you. This is not a random moment. It is on purpose and with purpose from God for your life.

Like many people, I have prayed for things, and when those things occurred, I questioned whether the response was real. I wonder if we believe what we pray for? If you pray for the opportunity and God aligns everything perfectly, trust that you're not dreaming. This is happening in your life. Do you second-guess your blessing? Hebrews 11:6 (NIV) says, "Without faith it is impossible to please God, because anyone who comes to him must believe that he exists and that he rewards those who earnestly seek him." When we make the requests, we must be ready to receive the reward.

There are a few things that I've discovered are necessary when embracing the moments God sends in our lives. Let's examine the biblical narrative of Peter and Jesus walking on the water. Matthew 14: 22-29 (NIV) says:

> Immediately Jesus made the disciples get into the boat and go on ahead of him to the other side, while he dismissed the crowd. After he had dismissed them, he went up on a mountainside by himself to pray. Later that night, He was there alone, and the boat was already a considerable distance from land, buffeted by the waves because the wind was against it. Shortly before dawn Jesus went out to them, walking on the lake. When the disciples saw him walking on the lake, they were terrified. "It's a ghost," they said, and cried out in fear. But Jesus immediately said to them: "Take courage! It is I. Don't be afraid. . . . Come," he said. Then Peter got down out of the boat, walked on the water and came toward Jesus.

This is a familiar story, and I'm certain you have heard it. But it gives us important signposts, some requirements, so we don't miss our moment.

Have courage. The first requirement is to have courage. Courage is the ability to do something when you are frightened. The disciples were afraid and didn't recognize Jesus walking on the water. Their fear limited their ability to embrace a significant moment. The fact that Jesus addressed it and told them to have courage indicates that fear keeps us from receiving God's best in our lives.

Second Timothy 1:7 says, "For God has not given us a spirit of fear, but of power and of love and of a sound mind." Fear is a spirit that limits your capacity. It cuts off your foresight. If you are going to embrace this moment, have the courage to believe God for what's possible. Jesus is not going to be on the water all night.

When you have courage, it causes you to imagine and think at another level from those around you. While they are thinking about staying afloat in their boats, you are thinking about embracing a moment beyond the confines of the boat. Courage is what separates you from others. Rollo May, the author of the book *The Courage to Create*, states the following regarding courage:

> Courage is not a virtue or value among other personal values like love or fidelity. It is the foundations that underlies and gives reality to all other virtue and personal values. The word *courage* comes from the same stem as the French word *Coeur*, meaning "heart." Thus just as one's heart, by pumping blood to one's arms, legs, and brain enables all the other physical organs to function, so courage makes possible all the psychological virtues. Without courage other values wither away into mere facsimiles of virtue.[1]

Without courage, other virtues are unsupported and become a weaker version of what is needed for you to live in the fullness of your moment. Courage causes you to come to the conclusion that if you are to embrace the moment, something radical has to happen. Peter realized that this was his moment, and if he didn't act now, it wasn't going to happen. Perhaps you are reading this knowing that everything is in place, but you've allowed fear to creep in and keep you in the confines of your comfort zone. It's time for you to make a decision. Stay in the boat of comfort, or get out of the boat and seize the moment.

Be convinced. The second requirement is to be convinced. Once Jesus said, "It is I," that was all Peter needed to hear. Whatever ambiguity or uncertainty that existed prior to that moment, it was resolved when He declared, "It is I." When you hear Jesus

---

1 May, R. (1975). *The Courage to Create*. New York: W. W. Norton and Company.

tell you, "It is I," the great I AM is saying to you, "I am in this moment." You will never embrace your moment if you are not convinced. I would have never accepted the call into ministry if I had not been fully convinced.

Jesus still speaks today to remind us that when moments come, He is in them. Often, people in our lives will doubt us, but you cannot be swayed by the opinions of people when you have clearly heard His voice utter, "It is I." Just because everybody heard Him say it doesn't guarantee that it will have the same impact on them. Peter was the only one willing to engage Him beyond the confines of the boat. Peter said, "If it's you, tell me to come to you on the water." And what happened next changed history forever.

Be committed. The third requirement is to be committed. Once Peter was convinced, the Bible says that he committed and left the boat at Jesus' invitation. Peter responded to the invitation, "Come!"

When you are committed, there are two fundamental things that will happen. First, you will be willing to walk away from what's comfortable. You are willing to detach from certain relationships and systems in order not to miss the moment. The second thing is that you realize the urgency of the moment. Peter teaches us to be willing to get to Jesus before He gets back in the boat. That's the window of time you are dealing with. Jesus was coming toward the disciples in the boat, but Peter's moment was out there on the water.

You can't be partially committed. You can't be half in and half out. Be fully committed. Peter became a water-walker because he was committed to full engagement to go where Jesus commanded. We often want Jesus to come to where we are, but true commitment means that we are willing to go where He is. He's out there on the water, not in the boat. Don't miss your moment hanging out with people with boat mentality. Boat mentality puts constraints on what's possible. People who are comfortable on the boat never reach the heights of water-walkers.

> The only thing sadder than a "never been" is a "could've been."

Be creative. The fourth requirement is to be creative. People who walk on water like Peter are those who operate outside the box. They are the creatives among us who keep pushing the envelope. Think about this for a minute. Peter dared to do something that had never been done before. No one other than Jesus had ever walked on water. When you are creative, you embrace the fact that your moment may be calling you into something that has no precedent. In the beginning, God created. God is a creator of beginnings, so don't be surprised if He calls you to start something or be something new.

God stepped out on nothing and made something. When God presented me with strategic moments, He was asking me to do things that had never been done in the spaces where I was. I had to embrace the reality that there is a creative side in all of us that pulls us beyond the norms of tradition and comfort.

You can say what you want to about Peter taking his eyes off Jesus and falling into the water, but you can't deny that he did walk on water. Don't allow people on the boat to criticize you because of your failures on the water. Remember that they had the chance but didn't have the courage, conviction, or commitment to do it themselves. You can't receive constructive criticism from people who have never constructed anything.

You can never know when opportunity will come into your life. But when it does, it's important that you have an awareness of the lessons I've shared in this chapter. Missing moments leaves us bitter and condemns us to live with unmet expectations. The only thing worse than a "never been" is a "could've been." When God sends you a moment, there is an expectation that you will enthusiastically embrace it and manifest every purpose God intended when He sent it. Moments come, and moments go. Be poised to take the next one.

QUESTIONS

1. What *kairos* moments have you taken advantage of? What happened?
2. What *kairos* moments have you missed? What happened?
3. How have you prepared yourself to respond to the opportunities God has given you?
4. How have your opportunities affected the lives of others?
5. Can you identify with Peter's experience of walking on water? If so, how?

3

EMBRACE OPPORTUNITY

By now you have a clear understanding of the significance of your moment of opportunity and how to walk in it. In this chapter, I want to help you embrace it. Yes, embrace it. When I accepted my assignment as a pastor, I had to realize that in order for me to be successful, I had to embrace everything that came along with it.

You don't get to determine what parts of the assignment you will embrace. When you are walking in complete purpose, brace yourself for all the things you expect, as well as the unexpected. If you don't embrace the opportunity, you will never become one with it, therefore you will never give full attention to the things necessary to make it work. Own the moment and be willing to do whatever it takes to assure that you produce at maximum levels.

Success is intentional. It doesn't just happen.

I've seen so many people walk into opportunities but never fully embrace them. This attitude produces a lackluster and apathetic engagement that stifles growth and hinders productivity.

ALL IN!

There is a word that governs how I embrace opportunity: *intentionality*. I have learned that success is intentional. It doesn't just happen. Be intentional and fully engaged. Once, I asked my staff in a team meeting to repeat the phrase *all in* if they felt fully engaged. This would reveal to me who was invested in the vision and who was simply working a job. The vast majority yelled, "All in!" but when I heard a couple say "in" rather than "all in," I knew that there was a disconnect. It didn't mean that they were bad people; it just meant they were honest about where they were and no longer had the passion to be connected.

Give people space to be honest. Some years ago, I shared with a group of leaders that when you receive a resignation letter from someone, they have resigned long before you get the letter. You cannot embrace what you are not connected to. Trying to hold on to people who are not fully invested is a disservice to them and you.

When the space shuttle took off, it had two rocket boosters attached. Once it reached a certain altitude, those two rocket boosters fell off. There was nothing wrong with the shuttle or the rocket boosters. They served their purpose and were not designed to fly in the shuttle's orbit. If they didn't release, they would have created drag and would have threatened the safety of the shuttle and caused it to miss its destination.

Just like those rocket boosters, some people are going to fall off. Don't get bitter or upset. Remember, they are not designed to fly in your orbit. Whatever your opportunity is, you and the people connected to you must be "all in" if you are going to be successful.

INFRASTRUCTURE

I'm an infrastructure guy. I realize that a lot of people like to enjoy the finished product, but it takes a strong infrastructure to assure sustainability of your vision. If you are going to fully embrace opportunity, learn to effectively manage it. There are four principles I want to share with you that you need if you are to realize your vision and dream. These four principles are the areas that must be managed properly: product, process, people, and profit. Let's carefully examine each of them and see how they assist you in embracing opportunity.

Product

First, let's discuss the product. The product is that thing you are attempting to do. It's your "what." For instance, Chick-fil-A franchised a successful business on the concept that everybody needs a change from eating hamburgers. The vision was to create a market for chicken sandwiches. This was new and the company had to invent a new cooking process, but the vision was successful because the product is clear. Chicken! Clearly identity what your product is. Within the scope of your vision, ask yourself, *What is the "what"?*

I've met so with many people who had great passion about doing something, but when pressed on the specifics of the "what," they were unable to clearly articulate it. Habakkuk 2:2 says, "Write the vision, and make it plain." If it is not clear to you, it will never be clear to anybody else. This is why it's important to be in purpose, because it is there that things are made clear.

Don't allow the term *product* to cause you to miss the point. Although I am using a term used by entrepreneurs, in this context the intent is to draw attention to the big idea you are trying to accomplish. There can be several variations of the product, but it remains the same. There can be chicken salads, chicken wraps, chicken strips, but the product is chicken. Chick-fil-A is clearly not in the beef business. The product is what everything centers around. The product communicates and makes the vision concrete.

I want to encourage you to think about your niche. In the scope of your vision, what is the thing that separates you from others? Remember what we discussed in Chapter 1. Your purpose solves a problem. Now, people who don't eat beef but who love sandwiches have a solution because of a product that meets their needs. Knowing the product, or "what," of your vision makes it easier to embrace opportunity.

Process

The second area that must be managed is the process. This is the area where I've seen many visions die. Lazy people despise process because they think vision just magically happens. Process is where the real work is.

Let's continue to use our illustration of Chick-fil-A. If chicken is the product, then the process raises a series of questions. Where will we get the chicken? How will the chicken get to the store? How will we deliver the chicken? Where will we get our potatoes to make fries? What is our branding strategy to market our chicken? How should our stores look? Where will they be?

I know you are probably saying, "Whew," but this is only the beginning of questions that must be examined and answered if the product is going to be successful. Where many people fail is that they have great visions but not a process, a method. I've seen people advertise an event with a flier and post it on FaceBook but not think about the processes that need to be in place for that thing to happen effectively and efficiently. Since this is a book on executing vision and understanding how things get done, let me share with you how process works with our team.

Currently, the first thing I do is bring the entire team together around a particular event. Whoever has responsibilities for that event in any way initially needs to be at the table. One of the benefits of meeting with your whole team initially is that it also eliminates redundancy. Nobody likes going from meetings to meet about the things they just met about.

In the past, I would cast vision in a vacuum or with a select few and then entrust them to go and share the vision and responsibilities with their teams. What I discovered is that it's best for everyone to hear it from the visionary firsthand, so there is no misinterpretation of what is being said.

Have the entire team at the table, because in real time they are able to share with me what I may have overlooked or how the vision might adversely affect an area they manage. For instance, if I'm planning a family conference and that week falls on the same week children are taking tests in school, it might not get the turnout I expected, because it conflicts with something I was unaware of. Having people at the table who can inform you of every possible area the vision will touch is essential is casting vision.

When I cast the vision, I want my facilities team there so they can know, for example, exactly how many chairs and rooms we might need. I have my technical team there to hear about our sound and lighting needs along with Internet connectivity. My media team is there to capture what they need to promote the event. My hospitality team is there so we don't drop any balls with our guests. Logistics are covered on all fronts.

You may say, "That's a lot of details," but I believe success is in the details. This is what separates highly successful organizations from mediocre ones. When you pay attention to details, you operate in a spirit of excellence, and people feel confident that you are properly managing your vision. Without this process, people might show up and there is nobody to run the sound, because you assumed there would be. Guests might be stranded at the airport because nobody thought to assign someone to be over transportation. If there is one thing that makes the shipping company UPS so successful it is the fact that they focus on logistics. Put all the questions on the board and allow your team to answer them so that nothing is left to chance. Who will do what, when, and how?

Allow me to say this about process. If you are serious about being effective in this area, approach it as a leader with a great deal of flexibility. You can't be successful if there is no room for redaction. Your team is your greatest resource. Listen to their suggestions, because they are on the ground and understand how the vision will impact their area of focus.

I listen attentively to my team and welcome their input. If you don't value the input of those around you, ask yourself the question, *Why are they on my team?* Allow those around you with creative gifts to sharpen and enhance your vision so that it is inclusive and successful. You can't allow pride to keep God's best from you.

I've seen so many leaders whose egos have prevented them from receiving advice or alternative solutions from people who serve under them. Wherever people are on the hierarchical totem pole, they have things to share that may be of great benefit. As a visionary, spend time listening. Neither you nor I have it all together.

Remain a constant student. Create opportunities where people can share truthfully without fear of retaliation. Jesus asked the disciples one day, "Who do men say that I am?" Create an environment of collaboration where you can cultivate teamwork. So often, we operate with hierarchical models where someone has to be over another to feel validated.

> Teamwork makes dreams work.

It's important when embracing opportunity that you promote a shared model of leadership. It is true that "teamwork makes dreams work." Your dream is too valuable not to invite the best and brightest minds to have input. One of the things to which I attribute my success as a leader is my willingness to listen to others around me and implement ideas that broaden the reach of the vision. Your vision can impact more than you ever imagined when you foster collaboration. This is where experiences are birthed.

People

The next area that must be managed is people. This is critical to the success of your vision, because it's always about relationships. People can make or break the vision. When Chick-fil-A hires people, there is a certain type of person they hire. They hire those who are consistent with their brand. Some of the most wonderful and kind people work there because they are on the frontlines delivering the product.

Once, I dropped my sandwich in the parking lot shortly after purchasing it. I went back into the store and explained what happened. With no questions asked, the person behind the counter gave me a new sandwich, then smiled and asked kindly if there was anything else I needed. Can you imagine the alternative to this? I could have been interrogated and told that I needed to purchase a new sandwich, but Chick-fil-A puts a premium on customer service and goes the extra mile to assure complete customer satisfaction.

The people who connect with your vision are just as important as the product of your vision. The culture and climate are set by the people. This is why you cannot have random people connected to your vision. They must be people who can represent you and your vision and represent you well. The people around you are a direct reflection of who you are. My mother always said that she could tell how we felt about ourselves by the people we hung around. I can tell what you think of your vision by the people you allow to be engaged with it.

One of the things we attempt to do at our church is train our staff and volunteers in customer service. When people have a bad experience with one employee or volunteer, it can sour the entire experience and cast a negative light on the entire organization. Make certain that the right people are aligned with your vision. In the Old Testament, a person would transfer their spirit to those who would carry the vision, as when Elijah gave his mantle to Elisha. People connected to your vision should not only embrace it, but they should share your spirit.

I think about what Psalm 133 says: "How good and pleasant it is for brethren to dwell together in unity! It is like the precious oil upon the head, running down on the beard, the beard of Aaron, running down on the edge of his garments." This powerful psalm is about people being in unison with a vision. Imagine this: The oil that's on the head flows down to the skirts of the garment. If you were to take a sample of the oil from the head and a sample from the hem, you would get a perfect match.

What we stand under is ultimately what we understand.

I often tell leaders that you can't have a nice pastor and a mean usher. It suggests that somewhere the oil went bad. What we stand under is ultimately what we understand. Make certain people who are connected to your vision understand what's important to you. Share with them your values and how important their attitudes and practices are to the organization. No matter how busy you are, be engaged with your team.

I love watching the show *Undercover Boss*. This show is about CEOs who go undercover to get a sense of how their companies are performing and also to gauge the morale of the people who work for them. It's always amazing to see how disconnected many CEOs are to the ground level inner workings of their organizations. Once they are made aware of the concerns, they can set out to make amends by fixing failing systems, procedures, and policies and also to increase morale among those who work for their companies.

We can get so busy that we lose sight of what really matters. When you spend time evaluating your vision and those close to it, you are able to distinguish between those who add value and those who are liabilities.

You can have the most powerful vision, but if you have the wrong people around it, it is dead on arrival. This is why Jesus "chose" His 12 disciples. His choices were not accidental; they were intentional. Spend time seeking God concerning the kind of people you should have representing your vision.

Profit

The fourth area that needs to be managed is profit. This is the endgame. It is less about money than it is about the fruit your vision will produce. Your profit, or fruit, is determined by your people, who are guided by your process, which is birthed out of your product. When all these things are in place, you produce at a high level. This is what the Lord requires of us. You don't have time to waste. This is why you are reading this book. No opportunities will be wasted. The full manifestation of your vision produces results. That's the profit.

No one on the team is larger than the vision.

Profit is measurable because it has a return on investment (ROI). Any vision worth its salt is measurable. When you measure results, it keeps you honest and allows you to constantly adjust and improve. If you are successful in managing these four areas, you will continue to trend upward.

In John 15:8, Jesus says, "Herein is my Father glorified, that ye bare much fruit." If what you do does not bear fruit, revisit these four areas and locate the problem. Once you locate the problem, be willing to do the things necessary in order to move the vision along. This is tough work. You cannot be consumed with the emotions of others. When making decisions, remember that nobody on the team is larger than the vision.

Embracing opportunity commits you to be invested in all areas of the vision. This is what makes you the leader you are. You cannot expect what you are not willing to inspect. You are not micromanaging. Rather, you are paying attention to the fine print of getting things done in order to assure that the vision comes to fruition in a way that glorifies God. Though you entrust the vision to the ideas and input of others, you are ultimately responsible for the outcome.

As a leader, you cannot just set the vision at a *high-level* and expect those within your organization to fill in the details. Provide directions that are crystal clear. Often, what some believe to be a lack of motivation among workers in an organization is actually a lack of direction. Vision must include direction.

Chip Heath and Dan Heath, authors of the book *Switch*, write, "Ambiguity is the enemy. Any successful change requires a translation of ambiguous goals into concrete behaviors."[1] Those who are committed to walking with you depend on you to provide the directions for their next steps.

Every single day I walk in my assignment, I thank God for the opportunity I have to represent Him. When you embrace opportunity, you are committed to providing all who engage your vision with an experience they will never forget. Positive experience drives people back to your vision. Perhaps this is why the line in

---

1 Heath, D., & Heath, C. (2010). *Switch: How to Change Things When Change Is Hard.* New York: Broadway Books.

the drive-thru at Chick-fil-A is always long. People enjoy not only the product but enjoy the experience that surrounds it.

When people come to our church, we want them to remember the experience from the parking lot to the pulpit. It doesn't matter how amazing your product is. If the experience is horrible, it will be a permanent label on you that will be detrimental to your growth. You've worked too hard to see your vision become manifest to lose sight of the experience surrounding it. Nothing should be left to chance.

RELATIONSHIPS OVER RULES

One of the most important lessons I've learned when embracing opportunity and managing vision is that I have to put relationship over rules. Rules are necessary in order to maintain order and structure; however, never become so legalistic with your vision that you are not willing to compromise for the sake of relationship. By no means does this suggest doing things that are illegal or unethical. What I am suggesting is that you develop an ethos within your organization where rules don't prevent needs from being met.

Being an effective manager will challenge you to make wise decisions. If a person is hungry and the food pantry is not open on the day they are hungry, is telling them to come back representative of your vision? Or should you have someone go across the street to get them a sandwich? Spending $5 of pocket change can salvage a relationship and speak volumes about who you are and how your vision touches peoples' lives.

When the woman with the issue of blood pressed her way to Jesus, she had a need. But the disciples were so concerned about rules and where they were going that they didn't recognize that someone had touched Jesus. Jesus noticed. He said, "Who touched me?" And their response is indicative of those who have yet to fully embrace opportunity and be invested in the vision. They said, "A lot of people are touching you." Then Jesus said something incredibly powerful: "Virtue is gone out of me." His sensitivity to the needs of people speaks to relationship beyond rules. He had a connection to people and their needs.

The woman had an issue of blood, and the rules said she was unclean. According to the rules, she should have never gotten that close because whoever she touched would also be considered unclean. Nevertheless, when Jesus says that something has gone out of him, it reveals a powerful lesson. When you put relationship over rules, the needs of people pull something out of you that causes you to stop and show compassion regardless of what the rules say.

People should leave us better than when they meet us.

The woman was made whole because of her faith. Notice that she engaged Jesus, and the end result was an experience of being made whole. People should leave us better than when they meet us.

As you embrace opportunity, make sure that your vision produces positive results anchored in positive relationships. Matthew 7:16 says, "You will know them by their fruits." All the time you spend preparing and investing in your dream means nothing if there is no fruit at the end of the day. Don't participate in labor without reward. That's slavery. When people engage your vision, there should be noticeable differences in their lives. We have a saying at our church that we declare with boldness and conviction: "You won't leave here the same way you came." We couldn't say that if we didn't put the work in every day to assure it.

CONCLUSION

Embrace opportunity and do the real work necessary to bring your vision to pass. You have the power as a leader to steward your vision and help those connected to you represent it properly. You get one chance to make a first impression. You can't always control how people will respond to your vision, but you can be intentional about making certain that you've done all the things necessary for them to have a positive experience.

Everything you do to make your vision come to pass should help make the world around you better. Robert F. Kennedy once stated, "The purpose of life is to contribute in some way to making things better."[2] In the same vein of thought, Martin Luther King Jr. said, "No work is insignificant. All labor that uplifts humanity has dignity and importance and should be undertaken with painstaking excellence."[3]

Regardless of the size of the vision or the work you are assigned to accomplish, when you embrace the opportunity with the right timing, your impact will be great. As you move forward in the pursuit of the manifestation of your vision, remember that opportunities come with unpredictable elements. If you are fully engaged and invested in a successful outcome, take seriously the principles we've shared in this chapter. Embrace opportunity with

---

2 https://www.goodreads.com/quotes/tag/make-a-difference.

3 https://www.goodreads.com/quotes/tag/make-a-difference.

the high hopes for what's possible. Embrace opportunity doing the work that promotes and cultivates an environment for future growth. Now is the time, and you are the person to do it.

QUESTIONS

1. What is your "product"?
2. What process have you established to take advantage of your opportunities?
3. Who are the people attached to your vision? Are they helping to move your vision forward or backward, or are they keeping it in neutral?
4. What is the endgame for your vision?
5. How will your vision make the world a better place?

4

DEVELOP A NOW CULTURE

One of the most vital things I've learned as a leader is the importance of the culture that any organization creates and cultivates. Culture speaks loud and clear. A NOW (No Opportunity Wasted) culture speaks to your values and determination not to waste any opportunity. Study.com says this about culture:

> Organizational culture works a lot like this. Every company has its own unique personality, just like people do. The unique personality of an organization is referred to as its culture. In groups of people who work together, organizational culture is an invisible but powerful force that influences the behavior of the members of that group.

The article also defines organizational culture:

> Organizational culture is a system of shared assumptions, values, and beliefs, which governs how people behave in organizations. These shared values have a strong influence on the people in the organization and dictate how they dress, act, and perform their jobs. Every organization develops and maintains a unique culture, which provides guidelines and boundaries for the behavior of the members of the organization.

Let's explore what elements make up an organization's culture.

Before people actually see and appreciate our work, they take note of the environment that produces it. I believe that we as leaders set the tone for the culture of those who work alongside us. In Acts 4:13, Peter shares with us how culture is contagious when referring to the disciples post-Pentecost. When the cynics and skeptics looked on the disciples with scorn and contempt, their own words confirmed the power of culture: "Now when they saw the boldness of Peter and John, and perceived that they were unlearned and ignorant men, they marveled; and they took knowledge of them, that they had been with Jesus."

BUILDING A NOW TEAM

When you begin moving into your assignment and building a support team, keep in mind the importance of developing the right culture. A NOW culture is one that is sustainable and productive. When our church began to grow, it was important to bring alongside the vision-effective staff persons who could assist in moving vision forward.

Staffing is one of the most important decisions of any business or organization. People ask me all the time about the criteria I've used in selecting the right people to bring alongside the work God was doing. Allow me to share with you the criteria I use. There are four traits that every person we employ, and who stays employed, must possess: character, competence, cadence, and capacity.

CHARACTER

I like to define *character* as behavior on display. It is at the top of the list when developing a NOW culture. People who are connected to your organization must possess this trait. If they don't have it, there will be significant damage to your vision. You can't expect people to be perfect because they're not, but you can raise a standard that demands people operate at high levels of character. When people have good character, they will not come to your organization with ulterior motives that undermine your vision. People with good character can be trusted.

Trust is not something easily given. You cannot afford to have people you cannot trust connected to your dream. I've seen organizations where distrust was prevalent. When distrust is present, it creates a toxic work environment that makes it nearly impossible to collaborate, because honesty must be present. We are not apt to openly share ideas and thoughts with people we don't trust, thus limiting the creative bandwidth among those responsible for stewarding the vision. To put it bluntly, it's difficult to build a team where there has been a violation of trust.

When it comes to character, there can be no compromise. I remember hearing a story that helped put this in perspective for me. One day, a beaver was preparing to cross a creek, and he saw a snake who was quite ill.

The snake said to the beaver, "Mr. Beaver, can you please carry me to the other side of the creek so I don't die here? I'm very ill and would appreciate your kindness."

"Oh no, Mr. Snake," the beaver replied. "If I do that, you are going to bite me and eat me."

The snake then replied, "I promise I won't eat you, Mr. Beaver. I'm so ill and just need help. Please, if you can find it in your heart, help me to the other side of the creek."

The beaver felt so sorry for the poor snake and reflected on what he felt was the right thing to do.

The beaver then replied, "Okay, Mr. Snake, I'll do it, but remember you promised not to bite."

The ill snake got on the beaver's back, and the beaver ferried the snake to the other side. As soon as they got to the other side, the snake bit the beaver, injecting him with poisonous venom. The beaver was in shock and unimaginably disappointed.

"Why did you do it? You promised if I helped you that you would not bite me!" exclaimed the beaver.

"I'm so sorry, Mr. Beaver," the snake replied, "but I am a snake. It's just in my nature."

This story changed my perspective and helped me understand that when people don't have character, nothing they say can be trusted because the nature of who they are will always prevail.

When I first became a leader, I was a softy like the beaver. My wife would often tell me that I give everybody a chance to my own fault. I overlooked the obvious and entrusted a lot of people who ultimately proved to have no character. I often would attempt to make excuses for them within the organization and deal with it by rearranging our team, shifting them to other departments, in hopes that the move would bring a cessation to the tensions the entire team was feeling.

If you have to constantly make excuses for poor character, there is a fundamental problem. I felt a need to salvage them in hopes that it—whatever it was—would magically get better. I learned the hard way that it didn't.

When cancer is discovered within the body, the physician doesn't consider relocating it to another part of the body. The ultimate goal is to get it out. A surgeon wouldn't remove cancerous cells from the lung and just relocate them to the brain. Unfortunately, this is how many leaders deal with people who are toxic within their organizations and businesses.

Developing a NOW culture demands that there be no compromise with those whose character compromises the integrity of your vision. Admittedly, I would start off giving people a 10 in hopes that they would never disappoint me, but many times they would end up at a 2, because their lack of character kept deducting points. These days, I give everybody a zero and allow them to earn points, therefore never putting myself in a position to be disappointed and never putting the vision in jeopardy.

COMPETENCE

Competence is simply defined as the ability to do something successfully or efficiently. Your vision can only be realized when you have competent people on your team. When competence is part of your culture, it raises the level of expectation regarding what you produce as well as the level of excellence associated with it.

A major threat to your vision is having expectations for those who lack the ability to produce it. This is a tough space to be in. As your vision begins to grow, your organization or business does as well. The people connected at one level must be able to maintain the level of efficiency, relevancy, and skill necessary to support the trajectory you are on. This is where difficult decisions have to be made.

You've got some good people who are loyal to your vision but no longer have the competency necessary to perform at the high level your vision demands. If you are going to develop a NOW culture, you are going to have to surround yourself with people who know what they are doing and do it well.

We often put people in positions because they are our friends, or we do them favors when they have fallen on tough times. It's when the demands of the vision are at their peak that we are able to see incompetence like never before. These are not bad people. The problem is that your vision and its demands for survival have outgrown the capabilities of those who historically were tied to it.

A culture of competence speaks to the value you place on the vision and how it impacts the lives of the people. Be mindful of how you position people who lack competence in certain areas but hold authoritative positions in the organization. In his book *Next Generation Leader*, Andy Stanley states,

> There is a difference between authority and competence. When we exert our authority in an area where we lack competence, we can derail projects and demotivate those who have the skills we lack. There is no need to become an expert in, or even to understand, every component of your organization. When you try to exercise authority within a department that is outside your core competencies, you will hinder everything and everyone under your watch. If

> you fail to distinguish between authority and competence, you will exert your influence in ways that damage projects and people. To put it bluntly, there are things you are responsible for that you should keep your nose out of.[4]

It's one thing to have competence, but it's another thing to have it properly positioned so that all the gifts and talents around you can flourish.

CADENCE

This area is incredibly important. I had the privilege of marching in the school band as a percussion section leader and also as a drum major. Cadence and rhythm are in my blood. When I blew the whistle, it was to establish the tempo or cadence for the band. After blowing the whistle, I would turn away from the band, look forward, and march. The expectation was that once the cadence was set, there was no need for me to look back, wondering if the band was right behind me because I knew they were in step with the tempo I had initiated.

Peter Drucker, author of *The Five Most Important Questions You Will Ever Ask About Your Organization*, writes the following concerning transformational leadership: "Lead from the front, don't push from the rear. The leader articulates clear positions on issues affecting the organization and is the embodiment of the enterprise, of its values and principles."[5]

---

4 [[There was a note that a citation was needed here.]]

5 Drucker, P. (2008). *The Five Most Important Questions You Will Ever Ask About Your Organizations*. San Francisco: Jossey-Bass.

When you are leading from the front, you are modeling the behavior that is expected from those who are following your lead. Your leadership model, once established, will then provide the footprints or blueprint of the design you seek to implement within your organization. If you push from the rear, those who follow you are then left to develop their own tempo instead of emulating your steps.

People who keep your rhythm are going to end up where you are going.

When you build a team, it is important that those around you keep your tempo. If you have to keep checking on them, wondering if they are keeping up with assignments or projects, you've got a cadence problem.

I've had numerous experiences with good people who just could not keep cadence. When I first started pastoring, my cadence was relatively slow. But now, with all the added responsibilities, my cadence has increased tremendously. You can't slow your cadence down to accommodate people who can't keep up. You've got a mission to fulfill and a specific time to get things done. By compromising cadence, you retard your progression toward destiny.

Don't apologize for your cadence. People who keep your rhythm are going to end up where you are going. Have the courage to release people who can't or won't keep up, because it's painful to set expectations on people who you know don't have the ability to live up to them. Remember, you are not marching in place. You are progressing forward toward a goal, and those on your team must be able to keep up.

CAPACITY

Capacity is defined as "the maximum amount that something can contain. The ability or power to do, experience, or understand something." People connected to you must possess capacity. They must exhibit the ability to grow with you. Some people lack the ability to go with you into new spaces. They lack capacity to adjust to your new normal. You are on a trajectory that will require more and more capacity. The higher you go, the fewer people are able to handle the air in the space where you will dwell. The higher you ascend, the less oxygen there will be.

You can't take everyone with you to the top. You just have to be selective about who can handle the elevated levels. When Jesus was transfigured on the mountain, He only took Peter, James, and John with Him. Matthew 17:1-8 (NLT) records:

> Six days later Jesus took Peter and the two brothers, James and John, and led them up a high mountain to be alone. As the men watched, Jesus' appearance was transformed so that his face shone like the sun, and his clothes became as white as light. Suddenly, Moses and Elijah appeared and began talking with Jesus. Peter exclaimed, "Lord, it's wonderful for us to be here! If you want, I'll make three shelters as memorials—one for you, one for Moses, and one for Elijah." But even as he spoke, a bright cloud overshadowed them, and a voice from the cloud said, "This is my dearly loved Son, who brings me great joy. Listen to him." The disciples were terrified and fell face down on the ground. Then Jesus came over and touched them. "Get up," he said. "Don't be afraid." And when they looked up, Moses and Elijah were gone, and they saw only Jesus.

These three, Peter, James, and John, were not perfect by any means, but it was clear to Jesus that they possessed capacity. They had enough faith and belief in who He was that they could handle the next level of revelation.

Jesus understood that you cannot always reveal the transformation God is bringing into your life to the crowd around you, because they may hinder the process if they do not have enough faith to believe that God can do it through you. These three disciples were able to see what Jesus would look like in the future and still understand Him in His present context. This is what capacity does.

JOURNEYING TOWARD DESTINY

A NOW culture does not happen overnight. It must be developed and cultivated before it can be fully formed, and you must be committed to the work necessary to bring it to pass. You cannot assume that it will emerge without the intentional engagement and equipping of others.

> Always invest in people who are willing to invest in themselves.

I spent years pouring into my staff in order to develop a NOW culture. When you are shifting from one way of existing to another, allow space for people to transition with you. These four Cs have become the criteria we've established for those who join our team, but I've also created opportunities for those who desire to grow so that their lives and work are congruent with these expectations.

Always invest in people who are willing to invest in themselves. These are the people who are salvageable to your team. If people are willing to get better, they will do better. As a result, your organization will be better.

As you journey toward destiny, it's important that you have the necessary relationships and connections. You cannot achieve your destiny without the right people who bring the right qualities with them. Jesus could have made it to His place of destiny alone, but He used wisdom in His pursuit. Jesus knew that He could make it to his destination sooner by having effective people on his team.

You don't have to a be lone ranger. The writer of Ecclesiastes 4:9-10 declares, "Two are better than one, because they have a good reward for their labor. For if they fall, one will lift up his companion. But woe to him who is alone when he falls, for he has no one to help him up."

CONCLUSION

Let me share with you a final point regarding the NOW culture. Surround yourself with people who are dedicated to their vocation. The people Jesus selected to be part of His ministry were busy in their own area of vocation when He found them. Matthew 4:18-22 (NLV) says,

> Jesus was walking by the Sea of Galilee. He saw two brothers. They were Simon (his other name was Peter) and Andrew, his brother. They were putting a net into the sea for they were fishermen. Jesus said to them, "Follow Me. I will make you fish for men!" At once they left their nets and followed Him. Going from there, Jesus saw two other brothers. They were James and John, the sons of Zebedee. They were sitting in a boat with their father, mending their nets. Jesus called

> them. At once they left the boat and their father and followed Jesus.

Jesus understood that those who excel in their area of work have the potential for greatness. Proverbs 22:29 declares, "Do you see a man who excels in his work? He will stand before kings; He will not stand before unknown men." People who excel in their professional work will be the ones who will be brought before great men and women. This is because people will recognize their work and speak well of them.

When people only do enough to get by, they will not be readily recommended by others and are not beneficial to a NOW culture. The people who go above and beyond the minimum required of them will be the ones who stand before greatness, and these are people you want to surround yourself with. This is how you can develop and sustain a NOW culture.

QUESTIONS

1. What kind of environment have you created for those who follow you? If necessary, what steps can you take to improve it?
2. How could you translate the story of the beaver and the snake to your own life experiences? What happened? What lessons did you learn?
3. In which of the four Cs (character, competence, cadence, and capacity) are you strongest? weakest?
4. How do you select your friends?
5. Evaluate your (NOW) culture on a personal and a professional level. What might you need to change to make your personal or professional culture more successful?

5

BURN WITHOUT BURNING OUT

You and your team may be intent on not wasting any opportunity, so you also have to consistently maintain that drive without letting up and burning out. I am often asked how I am able to maintain the schedule I do and produce without burning out. Over the years, I have been conscious of how many leaders experience burnout, and I've attempted to put it in a theological framework.

When God called Moses to confront Pharaoh and tell him to let His people go, it was nothing short of spectacular. Scripture says that the Lord spoke to Moses through a bush that was on fire but was not consumed. I've often wondered why God needed the theatrics of the burning bush to simply give Moses his assignment. I believe now that there is a powerful revelation attached to it.

The bush was burning but was not consumed by the fire. When God gives us our assignments, His desire is for us to have a burning for it but never to allow it to burn us out. Burnout occurs whenever we step outside of our original assignment.

God spoke with clarity when giving Moses his assignment: "Go tell Pharaoh to let My people go." I've seen so many people attempt to do too much and go well beyond the scope of their assignment and ultimately experience burnout. It doesn't matter what kind of theological language and label you ascribe to it, burnout is imminent in the lives of those who have extended themselves beyond what God called them to do.

When you do what God has called you to do and do only that, He will give you the grace to walk in your assignment without burning out.

If you are a progressive and passionate person like me, you see a need and immediately want to meet it. But, remember, you cannot "boil the ocean." This often puts many people in conflict because they feel obligated to "save the world." This is a messianic complex and is unhealthy. Recognize that God has placed other people on earth with assignments, too. You are not the only one. You shouldn't feel guilty concerning what is not your assignment.

In John 11, Lazarus was sick and died. When Jesus showed up at the tomb, He called Lazarus by name, and Lazarus was brought back from the dead and came out of the grave. A lot of people died the day Lazarus died. There were countless people in that cemetery who would have loved to have been raised from the dead. The fact is that they were not Jesus's assignment that day. Lazarus was the assignment. When you lock in on what God has called you to do and just do that, God will give you the grace to walk in your assignment without burning out.

Every single day I wake up, I wake up going to purpose. Although I am passionate about so many things, I cannot take my eye off the ball concerning my assignment and be all over the place. It is troubling to see so many people experience burnout. From pastors to corporate executives to hard-working everyday people. Burnout is no respecter of persons.

Before I share with you how to prevent burnout, let's first examine how to identify it. You cannot properly execute in your career if you are not aware of the signs. Though there are probably more clinical understandings or signposts related to burnout, I want to share with you what I've experienced in my life and in the lives of people I've worked with.

WEARINESS

The first sign is weariness. Now you may be saying that it's perfectly normal to get tired. I would agree with you. I'm not referring to just being tired from the day-to-day grind that comes from a good work ethic. Being tired is one thing, but being weary and constantly drained is another. Instead, I'm referring to the overwhelming sense of being drained whereby you are functioning without focus, when you are trying to pour out but have nothing left to give.

Some people have perfected the art of driving with their out-of-gas light on. They know exactly how many miles they have before the car runs out of gas and stops. Though it drives the passengers in the car crazy, these people are quite comfortable pushing the envelope.

When we push the envelope trying to perform at high levels all the time, we compromise our ability to be creative and productive. When you experience weariness, your patience is short, and things that would normally not bother you begin to infuriate you. Pay attention to that chronic feeling of being drained, because it will begin to affect every area of your life. From your personal relationships to your professional ones, the impact of weariness exacts a huge toll.

WORRY

The second sign is worry. You may be wondering what worry has to do with burnout. When we are constantly worried about process and outcomes, we never get to enjoy work. Purpose is not designed to be a taskmaster. Though worry is a natural part of being a leader, it's when we allow it to consume us that it becomes unhealthy and leads to burnout.

During my second year leading the Mount Zion Church, I was in a place of perpetual worry. This affected my ability to study and prepare messages, because I was distracted by every big and small thing that was occurring in the ministry. I was so consumed that I could not have conversations with friends without the things I was worried about invading the conversation.

Worry robbed me of sleep. I would wake up in the middle of the night in panic. I would be in bed, but I couldn't get my mind to stop racing. One night, God spoke to me concerning worry. In that still, small voice, I heard Him ask me to "give Him His church back." In other words, I was worried about things that He had the plan and power to handle. I was trying to fix it all, and that was not my responsibility.

WANDERING

The third sign of burnout is wandering. As a leader, you have a heightened sense of this. When people begin to drift, it is often an indication that they are overwhelmed and lack the capacity to deal with it. For some people, the easy solution is to disconnect and wander. Often, when we wander, we assign spiritual language to it to justify our instability. We say things like "God told me my season is up" or "The Lord has me on a journey," when in fact it's us, not God. Own when you are overwhelmed.

This humorous story helps make the point. A guy slept in one Sunday morning. His mother came in and woke him up.

"It's time to get up. You'll be late for church," she said. But he told her he didn't want to go to church.

She asked him why not, and he said, "Because I don't like that place, and I'm tired of those people. Why do I have to go?"

She leaned in a little closer and said, "Because you're 35 years old, and you're the pastor!"[1]

Let's face it, regardless of our positions, titles, or relationship with God, many of us have felt like jumping ship. The loss of passion is not always an indication that something is wrong with the organization. It could also mean that there are a host of unrelated

---

1 http://www.preachingtoday.com/sermons/sermons/2013/february/journey-of-hope.html.

things colliding in our lives, causing us to chuck it all. For some people, wandering seems to be the only real solution. Wandering is risky, though, because it has no particular destination. If there is no clear destination, you can waste precious time that could and should be used being productive.

WITHDRAWAL

The fourth sign is withdrawal. What makes this sign a little different than wandering is that you can be present but absent at the same time. This is when you've completely checked out. You can sit in meetings, but everything just sounds like the teacher's voice in Charlie Brown's classroom—unintelligible sounds. Withdrawal happens when you are on the job but locked in on social media rather than being fully engaged in what is happening at the moment.

When you experience withdrawal, it is a subliminal statement that says you don't have the energy to contribute to relationships, work, or the vision. I've seen people go to jobs every day that they have withdrawn from. I've witnessed people who were withdrawn even while they allowed others to pour into them. When you withdraw, you divest from the organization or work. There is no longer a desire to contribute to the success of the vision or to engage others, so you often end up isolated. This is a sure sign that you are on a collision course with burnout. You no longer have the energy. You no longer have the passion.

PREVENTING BURNOUT

Now that we understand the signs of burnout, let's discuss ways to prevent it. It's important to begin with this reminder: Stay in your assignment. Identifying, understanding, and properly managing your assignment is key to preventing burnout. When you find contentment in what you are supposed to do, you don't compete with what others are doing, and burnout won't compromise your assignment.

It's also important that you have a good assessment of the tools necessary to complete the assignment. The Bible says in Luke 14:28 (NLT), "But don't begin until you count the cost. For who would begin construction of a building without first calculating the cost to see if there is enough money to finish it?" Counting the cost is essential to preventing burnout. It prevents unnecessary and stressful surprises. People often burnout because they didn't pay attention or account for the details.

How we handle adversity is important as well. When you are focused on your assignment, you cannot focus on the constant attacks that come with it. Your ability to manage adversity will determine how well you avoid burnout. Adversity is designed to distract you from the completion of your assignment. When you become consumed with the wrong things, it can put everything you've worked for at risk.

There is a story of a man driving to a job interview. This was the final interview, and he was all but assured the job. This interview would seal the deal. While driving, a fly got into his car. It kept swarming and buzzing. It created such a stir that the driver began swatting the fly, trying to kill it.

After several attempts, the man's rage grew worse. He started swatting harder trying to stop the swarming fly until his frustration took his focus off the road. Ultimately, he lost control of the car, ended up in a ditch, and missed his interview. And because he missed the mandatory interview, he was denied the job. He lost everything he had hoped for because he was so intent on swatting a fly.

When we are experiencing attacks, we can't take our eye off the goal to focus on the flies that frustrate us. What flies are you swatting? What things have caused you to take your eyes off the goal? Don't allow adversity to rob you of what God has for your life. If only that man had just let the window down!

One final key to preventing burnout is managing achievement, or how you measure success within your assignment. If you are like me, you are a high achiever. What I have learned is that you have to celebrate the small wins rather than always waiting on the big ones. Part of growth is progress. We often complain and stress about things not reaching the level we envisioned. Sometimes, just pause and be thankful that things are moving in the right direction.

So what if you were expecting 100 people to show up at your event? If 50 came, don't be down on yourself. Fifty is better than 25. You are not lowering your bar by celebrating small steps. You are recognizing that some level of accomplishment has occurred, and that alone should keep you striving toward higher heights rather than viewing yourself as a failure. Winston Churchill once stated, "Success is not final, failure is not fatal: it is the courage to continue that counts."[2]

I used to be so hard on myself. I would be consumed with why I didn't meet certain benchmarks, and it would torment my mind. I had to come to the realization that "Rome was not built in a day." Perhaps you should take a moment and think about all the small successes you have under your belt and stop being so hard on yourself.

---

2 https://www.goodreads.com/quotes/tag/success.

REFUELING STRATEGIES

Perhaps you are reading this chapter and it has struck a chord with you, because burnout is a current reality for you. I want to share with you strategies to help you resolve burnout and refuel so you can continue on the path of destiny. I've found these principles helpful in my own life.

Recognition. Acknowledge that you need help. You cannot allow yourself to be filled with hubris and refuse to be humble enough to seek help. We often remain burned out because our pride won't allow us to be honest concerning our need for help.

If you cut yourself at home, you might attempt to find a band-aide that you can apply to stop the bleeding. But if you are stabbed, there is nothing in your medicine cabinet that can help. You need to call 911. By calling 911, you have acknowledged your limitation as well as the medical professionals' ability to assist you. You will only acknowledge your need for God to assist you when you accept your inability to help yourself. There is nothing wrong with declaring you are at the end of your own resources and need divine intervention.

If your faith is awake, you can go to sleep.

Rest. This is an area that I've struggled with for years. I could find myself lying in bed in the posture of rest but not resting. My mind would not slow down, therefore I was working while I was supposed to be sleeping. We all need to appreciate what it means to rest. Jesus thought so much of it, He declared in Matthew 11:28 (NLT), "Come to me, all you who are weary and carry heavy burdens, and I will give you rest." You cannot burn the candle at both ends and expect to be productive. It's completely unhealthy not to get proper rest.

Before I could properly rest, I had to realize its purpose. Rest is where I refuel. The Lord tells us in Psalm 23 to lie down in green pastures. The psalm paints a vivid picture of restoration and renewal. You can't go and go and go and expect to operate at optimal levels. No matter how demanding your schedule, carve out time to rest. When you rest, you are completely trusting in God's ability to sustain you and your work while your hands are not on it.

One of the most fascinating stories in the Bible is when Jesus was in the storm with the disciples. He got a pillow and went to sleep in the rear of the boat. The disciples were panicking when the storm became so fierce, but Jesus was asleep. Frightened, the disciples woke up Jesus. I imagine that they excitedly told him what he could easily observe himself. The storm was raging, and they were afraid. After a rebuke of their faithlessness, Jesus brought calm to the storm by saying, "Peace be still." The fact that He was asleep during the storm is a lesson for all us concerning the power of rest. If your faith is awake, you can go to sleep.

Restoration. As you pour yourself out for the benefit of others, allow yourself to be poured into. David says in Psalm 23 that "He restores my soul." Personal retreats are a necessity. My speaking and preaching schedule involves eight weekly services at my church, an average of two weekly speaking engagements around the world, a Tuesday morning prayer call where I present a devotional message, and a daily Periscope.

In the midst of this rigorous speaking schedule, my family obligations and staff, board, and other meetings consume a great deal of my time. Consequently, I have to be strategic about providing for rest and restoration in my schedule. I plan two to three days a month to get away from the hustle and bustle and allow my mind, body, and spirit to be poured into. I have a friend with a similar schedule who takes one day a week, one week a month, and one month a year away.

With the demands of my life, it would be impossible to produce results without restoration. I have found it helpful to go to the beach or to the mountains and just be still. I disconnect from social media, my laptop, and all work-related things and allow God to fill my spirit again.

I admit, though, that I have not been completely faithful in this area. When I meet with my team concerning my schedule, we often are scrambling to find the available days for me to get away. What I am learning is that you have to schedule those days for restoration, so when requests emerge, you are unavailable. But I have been guilty of compromising those much-needed days by filling them with events or answering invitations. Though I was blessed to be able to be a blessing to a conference or a person at their request, the personal toll was great.

Restoration is about self-care. It's something many of us don't do a good job of, especially those of us in the helping professions. You only have one you. Your family has only one you. Make you a priority. Going to the spa, sitting in the park, lying on a beach, or riding a trail can be rewarding. When we take care of ourselves, we are in a better position to pour out to others.

I was at a party and saw a pitcher being used to pour punch. Though it was aesthetically beautiful, it had a functional flaw. It had a small crack at the base. Though it was pouring out into smaller cups, much of the punch leaked onto the table and was wasted. I thought about how many of us look the part but don't recognize the small cracks in our lives that prevent us from giving maximum output. This is why things are such a mess. Take time to step away from it all, and allow yourself to be poured into. The mentor needs to be mentored. The teacher needs to be taught. The pastor needs a pastor. The supporter needs support.

Regeneration. You can start fresh again. When you have been regenerated, new ideas, visions, and concepts begin to emerge. Your creativity is recharged, and you are able to operate at full throttle. Regeneration positions you to remain relevant. Your vision doesn't get stale. I have received some of the most awesome and innovative ideas during times of retreat. Whether attending a conference listening to cutting-edge thinkers or meditating alone with God, I've been able to absorb ideas that helped take my vision to the next level.

God wants us to live full lives, and after we have completed our assignments, we should be whole.

The thing you are attempting to accomplish needs you to be at an optimal level of performance. The world is constantly changing, and the need for what you have to offer must adapt to meet those changes. When you are regenerated, you are ready to take on the world. You are ready to execute with intentionality, focus, and energy.

DON'T LOSE SIGHT

Burnout is an enemy of progress, and it is important that you remain aware of how it can sneak up on you. As you maximize every moment of every day, make certain that you take the necessary steps to prevent it from hindering your destiny from coming to pass. As a motivated leader, there is a tendency to think things can't be done without you. I assure you that if you were in the hospital or in the grave, things would carry on without you.

God loves us so much that He doesn't want to see us self-destruct. If you will not rest voluntarily, it will happen involuntarily. There are a variety of adverse health issues that could arise when you don't take care of yourself. Whatever you are attempting to accomplish, it's not worth your blood pressure, a heart attack, or truncating your life. At the end of the day, it means nothing if you heal the world but end up broken.

God wants us to live full lives, and after we have completed our assignments, we should be whole. If you don't lose sight of what's important, you'll be in position to live into a culture that wastes no opportunity.

QUESTIONS

1. Have you ever experienced burnout? What happened?
2. How can your faith prevent burnout or bring you out of burnout?
3. How do you refuel?
4. How does Psalm 23 speak to burnout?
5. What could you do to help other people who may be experiencing burnout?

6

THE ART OF ESTABLISHING NOW RELATIONSHIPS

Establishing a NOW culture means cultivating NOW relationships. One of the most important things we could ever do is understand and be intentional about establishing healthy relationships. I've seen incredibly gifted people who had poor relationship skills. Our ability to maintain healthy relationships can impact the work we are attempting to accomplish, and any relationships that we establish must help propel us toward the fulfillment of our destiny.

We are wired for relationships.

I wanted to include this chapter on relationships because our relationships are a reflection of who we are. Our values, character, dreams, and hopes are intertwined with the relationships we allow ourselves to be part of.

Imagine just for a moment stepping away from the thing you want to do and focusing on the person you want to be. That person has needs that can only be met within the context of healthy relationships. Although you may think you don't need relationships, the truth is that we are wired for relationships.

I believe that when we operate in isolation, apart from human companionship, it is not healthy. Genesis 2:18 states, "And the LORD God said, 'It is not good that man should be alone; I will make him a helper comparable to him.' " God knew in the beginning when He created humanity that companionship would be a vital part of our existence. Relationships were established before anything else on earth, including the church, was instituted. God desires for our relationships to be a priority in our lives. The key to having healthy relationships is ensuring that the relationships you seek to build are with those people who can be comparable helpers to your destiny.

There is a direct connection between our relationships and destiny. When you look at the story of Jonah, it represents someone who is out of the will of God but is embraced on a ship with others whose lives are put in jeopardy as a consequence. When we allow people in our lives who are not in proper alignment with the will of God, we compromise our own dreams. Jonah received clear and concise instructions from God but chose to run. He went down to a place called Tarshish. Whenever a person runs from responsibility and purpose, it is always a trip down.

Jonah found a ship and paid the fare, which unveils another revelation. There is always a ship waiting to ferry people who are out of God's will. Perhaps it is a friendship, fellowship, or relationship. Whatever "ship" it is, it will ultimately be a hardship. If you see yourself like the mariners on the ship, you are able to see how significant relationships are. When we allow people on board in our lives, we have to take responsibility for some of the things that may occur as a result.

We all know that the storm that occurred was sent by God to get Jonah back in purpose. Whether Jonah was on the ship or on land, something would have occurred to get his attention. One of the most interesting things that happened in this story is that when the sailors realized that what they were going through was the result of being in relationship with a rebel, they asked Jonah what to do. The Bible says that Jonah informed the men that if they threw him overboard, the storm would stop. After receiving the news, the men rowed even harder to make it work. They resisted doing what Jonah said. Perhaps they didn't want to believe it.

When a person tells you the truth, learn to believe it. Jonah told them the truth, but they figured after hearing it that maybe there was some alternative way to get around it. When people show you who they are, believe them. You can't continue making excuses for dysfunction. The longer you keep Jonah on board, the longer you are going to stay in that storm. John 8:32 says, "And you shall know the truth, and the truth shall make you free."

People will often tell you that they mean you no good in word and deed. When they tell you their issue, learn to believe them instead of attempting to see something deeper in the situation.

They are giving you the truth and a fair warning. Consider this as your way of escape. When people reveal to you that they are a threat to you, provide them with the exit they asked for the first time.

> "When someone shows you who they are, believe them the first time."
> —Maya Angelou

Stop trying to save people that only God can save. Attempting to hold on to them and to the relationship can mean sudden death for you. Don't go through life with a messianic complex. According to psychologists, a messianic complex is a psychological disorder in which a person believes that he or she is a savior today or will be in the near future. There is only one Jesus, and you're not Him.

When you believe you are the savior for everybody, you put yourself in the direct way of the discipline meant for someone else. It is like when a child is getting a whooping and he runs toward you. If you don't move out of the way, you'll get his licks. Don't stand in the way of the discipline other people are receiving because of their own disobedience.

There are many of us who believe that it's our purpose in life to save other people. But when somebody is running from God and out of His will, there is nothing you can do. That person has to work that out with God. The reason why you can't get out of that messy storm and *drama-filled* relationship is because you have convinced yourself that it's your responsibility to row even harder to make it work. Don't fall for that trick. You may row, but this won't be "row, row, row your boat gently down the stream."

What starts out as a thunderstorm can turn into a hurricane in an instant. That's why it's important to make the right decision.

COMMITTING TO SOMEONE WHO WON'T COMMIT TO GOD

One of the signs of a dysfunctional relationship is when you commit to someone who refuses to commit to God. Jonah is the problem. When the problem tells you it's the problem, be willing to throw it overboard. I know for many of you that sounds so cruel and unloving, but if you attempt to aid and abet fugitives running from God, you will get caught in the vortex of their consequences.

The sailors did eventually throw Jonah overboard. I've learned this in personal and professional relationships. When you throw people overboard, you are actually releasing them into their destiny. When Abraham gave Lot an exit strategy out of his life, he didn't throw him away but gave him a plan to live life forward. Genesis 13:8-9 says,

> So Abram said to Lot, "Please let there be no strife between you and me, and between my herdsmen and your herdsmen; for we are brethren. Is not the whole land before you? Please separate from me. If you take the left, then I will go to the right; or, if you go to the right, then I will go to the left."

When Jacob and Laban had their final meeting, they were amicable in their time of departure, and Laban said to Jacob, "May the Lord watch between you and me when we are absent one from another" (Genesis 31:49). Learn how to pray God's blessing over people and then turn them over to the Lord.

God prepared a big fish to catch Jonah at the exact location where he was thrown overboard. Jonah is not your responsibility. God will deal with and take care of Jonah. Protect your ship at all cost, because it is the thing that ultimately ferries you to your destination. The good news in the story is that Jonah was vomited up by the fish on dry ground and, ultimately, got right with God. Allow God to deal with your Jonah. You are not God. There is only one Lord and Savior, and only God can save, set free, heal, and deliver. Stop serving as a surrogate savior.

You can't make the world right by being in relationship with the wrong people.

The psychological community has a term for this type of behavior: hero complex. The hero complex, also known as hero syndrome or superhero complex, is an inordinate desire to help others. It is a compulsion to help make the world right. It is a compulsion, so it is unhealthy.

You can't make the world right by being in relationship with the wrong people. The assignment you have been called to requires more than people who will follow you and get on your ship. In order to get to your place of destiny, you can only carry those in your relationSHIP who share your God-given destination.

Just because they don't belong on your ship does not mean they do not have a destiny for their lives. It just means they are not going in the same direction you are traveling. Allowing them to remain on the ship with you will only bring about storms you were not designed to handle.

As you look at the predicament of those who are managing the ship, understand that they are skilled at the art of travel. Therefore, they are accustomed to navigating the ship through storms. But, in the story of Jonah, the storm was too much for them, because it was not a storm they had been trained to face.

Remember, only God can deal with people who are not supposed to be traveling to your place of destiny. God loves them more than you can ever love them. Saint Augustine, the great Christian theologian, once stated, "God loves each of us as if there were only one of us."

God knows everything about you, down to how many hairs you have on your head. He says in Luke 12:7, "But the very hairs of your head are all numbered. Do not fear therefore; you are of more value than many sparrows." If God is that detailed-orientated about your being, He can deal with your personal issues.

God is God enough to deal with Jonah. This is above your ability. Once you release him, the Bible says that the Lord prepared a fish to swallow up Jonah. God didn't let him go under and drown, although Jonah surely must have thought so. God was concerned about him and was determined to get him to his destination. God's got Jonah. Jonah will make it, and you will, too. When you met Jonah, he wasn't ready to obey and follow God's assignment for him. But by the time we get to Chapter 3, the word of the Lord comes to Jonah a second time. After going through the belly of the fish, which represents self-reflection and repentance, he finally got there. On dry ground. Jonah went on to be successful, even though he wasn't happy about it.

I share that story with you because I've seen so many people retard the progress of their dreams and destiny because of poor decision-making regarding relationships. Often, our relational experiences find their way into other areas of our lives. If we've been hurt personally, we often transfer that pain into professional relationships. This transference hinders our ability to fully trust, because we become guarded and, in some cases, distant from those we work with. The devil has a deep desire to frustrate our relationships so that we become cynical and jaded. It is God's desire that our relationships are positive vertically (with Him) and horizontally (with others).

SETTING AND KEEPING STANDARDS

For years, I've had the privilege of traveling the world teaching on relationships. I've discovered that people are interested in getting them right. If you want your relationships to be successful, set and maintain standards. This is where many people fail. We find ourselves feeling guilty for placing standards on who we allow in our lives. There are certain standards that must be met prior to building a home or buying a car, or there will be no transaction.

If there are standards in most areas of life, why not set standards on who can be in relationship with you? But you will never set standards if you don't know your value. The more expensive the home you purchase, the more standards have to be met to qualify for the mortgage. When you understand that your dream is not cheap and what God is doing in your life carries great value, you will never allow someone to treat you like you are on discount.

Your values and your expectations in relationships are non-negotiable. You may have people who tell you that you are being unrealistic, but hold your position, even if it means you remain by yourself longer than others. There is a reason why a Rolls Royce stays on the showroom floor longer. Its value assures that, ultimately, a special kind of person will purchase it. It doesn't matter how many cars of lesser value fly off the showroom floor, the Rolls Royce holds its position and refuses to discount, because it's confident that the right person will emerge.

Whether you see yourself as a Rolls Royce or some other car of value, hold to your standards. It's best to hold your value and be alone longer than to become what amounts to a relational rental car. Rentals have too many drivers and too many miles. I think you get the point.

When you think of your standards in relationship, make a list and stick to it. Psalm 37:4 (KJV) says: "Delight thyself also in the LORD: and he shall give thee the desires of thine heart." God allows us to request those things that are in our heart as long as they line up with His Word. Your desires can range from physical standards to spiritual. Some people have certain intellectual standards. Others have certain health or emotional standards. Where you are going in life will determine the standards of those you plan to take with you. If you have a list of ten things, you don't have to settle for seven out of ten.

Back to my automobile illustration. If you desire a BMW 7 Series, fully loaded, you want only that. If they tell you it's on backorder and they have a 5 Series ready to go right now, you have a choice: Settle for the 5 Series because you want to drive now, or wait on what you desire. If you settle, you might get a great car, but you will always be comparing it to what you wanted.

The same applies in our relationships. The worst thing you can ever do is settle and go through life dreaming about what could have been had you simply waited. The standards you set gives people an indication of the value of your vision.

BOUNDARIES

Another key area to consider in relationships is boundaries. Setting proper boundaries helps to manage our expectations. No relationship can be healthy without clear understanding of boundaries.

When I was growing up, my mother shared a story with me in real time. Her response to certain friendships I had and how I interacted with them still speaks to me today. Imagine a house with a porch. That house also has a large front yard with a fence separating the property from the street. Each of these areas represents a boundary in my relationships. Some people would come to visit me, and my mother would say, "Go out there on the other side of the fence and talk to them, and close the gate behind you." Others were permitted in the front yard only, while some were granted access to the porch. Very few were invited into the house.

The level of access you give people in your life is predicated upon trust. In this day of social media, I'm amazed at how we allow people access into the "living room" of our lives who have not proven they can be trusted. Identify your "gate" relationships and those who you allow on the "porch." All relationships are important; they just serve different functions. When we set proper boundaries in our relationships, we prevent ourselves from needless pain.

COMMUNICATION

Communication is another key area of healthy relationships. This area challenges many people because they lack basic communication skills. If you are going to have sustainable relationships, you must be able to have conversation about your wants, needs, likes, dislikes, hopes, and dreams. I've often been amazed at how people can live in the same house for 20 years and wake up one morning convinced they don't know the other person anymore. Somewhere in the relationship, they stopped communicating.

Because you are constantly changing, it will be necessary to maintain open lines of communication with those you are in relationships with. Communication means nothing where there is no transparency. There must be a willingness to be open and honest about where you are and what you are feeling. If you don't communicate, people make assumptions and will attempt to engage you based on those assumptions. This is why relationships can be frustrating. People are answering questions you never asked.

If you are in healthy relationships, share where you are going and not let it intimidate the people in your life. People who are genuinely connected to you are not threatened by your dreams. They are actually inspired. I meet so many people who say that they have had to truncate their vision for fear it would run someone away. Never downsize your vision to accommodate people who are intimidated by what God is doing in your life. One of the true signs of authentic friends is that they can celebrate your happiness and the fulfillment of your dreams whether it involves them or not.

Growing up, I used to hear the statement "Game recognizes game." When entering into NOW relationships, connect with people who challenge and inspire you, not those who constantly drain you. Proverbs 27:17 says that "iron sharpens iron." When you are a progressive person, you are only intrigued or interested in connecting with people who are progressive. Progressive people are drawn to people who "get it.

Some people come into your life for a reason and others for a season.

"Relationships work best when other people can identify with the demands of your schedule and life. They also work best when people can easily assimilate into your life and you into theirs without causing disruption to the things that made you successful in the first place. Developing a NOW relationship requires a great deal of prayer and strategic decision-making.

SEASONS

Understanding seasons is so important. Some people come into your life for a reason and others for a season, so be okay with that. As you grow, some people will disconnect from you. Seasons change. As I mentioned earlier, the NASA space shuttle had two rocket boosters that would fall off after the shuttle was launched. They were designed to fall off at a certain altitude, because they were not designed to fly in the shuttle's orbit. Some people have to fall off or else they will abort your mission to your destination. One of the mistakes I made early as a leader is I allowed people to stay beyond their season.

When I was a child, the older people would always tell us about "leaving the right way." So many people create unnecessary tension and taint their reputation because they burn bridges. They don't understand that a season has passed. To just leave because of frustration or a host of other reasons is not justification for not having a conversation with persons who have poured into your life. The way you leave a relationship speaks to how you valued it. Don't get so caught up in your emotions that you forget to take time and honor the previous relationship and explain your next move. Even if they don't agree, at least you honored them enough to say something.

When you move on in relationships, move on. A lot of people become histrionic and recount the past over and over. The Bible says that God is doing a new thing, and NOW it shall spring forth. You can't spring if you cling. Don't demonize your past relationships to justify your new one. If your new relationship cannot stand on its own, perhaps you need to take a closer look at why you are entering the relationship.

Recently, I had an interesting experience while traveling. I often go to two or three cities in a week's time. This particular week, I had preached in three cities back to back. After returning to my hotel room late one night, I realized that my key didn't work. I was upset and went downstairs to make my complaint. I was tired and frustrated and just wanted to lie down.

Once I told my long story, the look on the desk clerk's face was one I will never forget. She said, "Sir, this is not the Hilton. This is the Marriott." At that moment, it hit me that I had the key from yesterday still in my pocket. I was trying to open today's door with yesterday's key. This is what many people do in relationships, but you can't walk into your destiny using an apparatus from another season in your life.

RELATIONSHIPS REQUIRE WORK

Relationships don't happen overnight. They require work. Consider where God is taking you, and give this area serious attention. How we approach relationships ultimately determines how people interact with us.

I know a lot of brilliant people with high IQs, but they have underwhelming relationship skills or poor EQ, emotional intelligence. Our emotional intelligence is a huge factor in how we produce in our lives. How we handle conflict, correction, and consequences gives others insight into our emotional bandwidth. When our insecurities take the lead in our decision-making, we compromise our ability to be invited to certain spaces where significant decisions are made.

I've seen people categorized, labeled, and even stigmatized because of their inability to be patient and let relationships take their course. On jobs right now, there are co-workers who have unanimously agreed that someone is difficult to work with. In more than a few of these cases, the person in question is always the last to agree with their assessment. The whole staff can't be wrong. All the people you've dated who have a similar concern regarding you can't be wrong. Even if it's not all true, there is some truth hidden in their concerns.

What real leadership does in those moments is not anchored down in rebellion. Rather, it seeks ways to communicate and reconcile issues that prevent productivity. Immaturity pouts, disconnects, and blames everybody. Maturity is objective, connects, and accepts responsibility. Maturity speaks from a place of courage, and it takes real courage to confront areas in our lives that need work. You cannot fix what you are not willing to face. If you are not willing to face your shortcomings and position yourself to interact with others in a positive way, you will inevitably be isolated personally and professionally. You have too much to offer and receive from others to allow failed relationships to prevent your vision from coming to fruition.

If you are going to develop NOW relationships, engage in self-assessments and overcome fear. It is nearly impossible to have healthy relationships that are based in fear. Fear-based relationships operate out of "what could happen." Fear that they might be unfaithful. Fear that they might not appreciate my gift. Fear that they might fire me. Fear causes us to hold back and walk on the proverbial eggshells in the relationship. One of my favorite Scriptures is 2 Timothy 1:7: "God has not given us a spirit of fear, but of power and of love and of a sound mind."

Fear is nothing more than **F**alse **E**vidence **A**ppearing **R**eal. It is counterproductive and should have no place in your life and relationships. First John 4:18 says, "There is no fear in love; but perfect love casts out fear, because fear involves torment. But he who fears has not made perfect in love." The adjective *perfect* in this passage in the Greek is the word *teleios*, which means full-grown, fully realized, of full age, or mature. When your relationships are guided by fear, it is a sign that there is immaturity within the relationship.[1]

Perfect love is powerful. Imagine if you had an innate fear of snakes, and every time you saw one you were terrified. Now imagine if you saw your young child walking unaware in the direction of a snake coiled ready to strike. Every fiber in your body would react to save your child. You would thrust yourself between the snake and your child to save his life by any means necessary. In that moment, the love for your child overshadowed the fear you had for the snake. That's perfect love.

ORGANIC

Let me share one final thought on NOW relationships. In order for relationships to have sustainability in your life, they must be

---

1 https://www.blueletterbible.org/lang/lexicon/lexicon.cfm?Strongs=G5046&t=KJV.

organic. I love eating organic foods because they don't contain artificial preservatives. These preservatives make food unhealthy.

When relationships are organic, you don't have to consistently create artificial, and in many cases superficial, preservatives to sustain them. When people want to be around you, it's organic. If you need an event or a gimmick for them to be around you, it becomes forced. Though they may come around, it's only temporary.

When I've had relationships that were no longer organic, although it was painful to admit, they had run their course. It was best to let them go so that I would no longer be putting people in a space they genuinely didn't want to be in. Let's face it, people do what they want to do and go where they want to go. When it's organic, you know it; and when it's not, accept it, move on, and establish new relationships.

QUESTIONS

1. Positively or negatively, how have your relationships affected your purpose?
2. What boundaries have you established in relationships? Did those boundaries work?
3. Have you ever held on to a relationship too long? What happened?
4. Have you ever cut off a relationship? What happened?
5. How does God work through our relationships to achieve purpose?

7

NOW COLLABORATION 2.0

One of the most important lessons I have learned as a leader is that solo leadership is antiquated and ineffective. There are many people who still attempt to get things done only to end up frustrated, because they are unable to get buy-in from others. Or when they do, their mission and message get lost in the process.

This is an area I am passionate about. My passion stems from seeing so many people and organizations have great ideas but remain unable to get people connected to what they have to offer. Have you ever wondered why you can have an incredibly resourced and necessary (in your mind) event for the community but only a handful of people show up? There are several reasons this occurs, and I will share with you how to get people excited about your vision and how to get buy-in from key stakeholders in the community. It all has to do with collaboration.

MOVING BEYOND THE NEED FOR PERSONAL RECOGNITION

Let's first take a hard look at the problem. I believe it is imperative to understand how and why things prevent collaboration before you embrace the solutions necessary to bring about effective change. One day, I sat in a meeting with colleagues debating why it was so hard to get churches and pastors to come together across the city. One of the elder pastors of the city spoke with piercing wisdom by suggesting the challenge was figuring out who should be in charge. That statement remains with me to this day.

One of the enemies of collaboration is moving beyond our desires for personal recognition. When positions, titles, affirmation, and personal accolades get bigger than the actual work being done, we miss out on NOW moments that could impact the lives of others. When jealousy, insecurity, and grandstanding are present, it becomes increasingly difficult to work together toward common goals.

One of the prerequisites Jesus gave to those who would engage His vision in the earth was denying self. Mark 8:34 says, "Whoever desires to come after Me, let him deny himself." Don't stand in the way of your own vision. Executing your vision requires it to be larger than you and your personal self-interest. You cannot micromanage vision. You can't hold on to every project and idea without releasing it into the hands of others who are able to bring more creativity and enhancement.

BRING THE RESOURCES TO THE PEOPLE

In most cities, you have a plethora of resources, but they exist in silos. I am blessed to lead the largest church in the state of Tennessee. To my amazement, there are programs that seek to provide resources to our congregation, but they have never attempted to contact me or engage the ministry personally. The strategy of many of these organizations is "Come to us" rather than "We will come to you." You can have an amazing vision, but if you don't move beyond where you are, it will never impact the persons it is intended to reach.

True collaboration is about bringing resources to people, but it's also about bringing people to the resources. This came through trial and error for me as a leader. You can unwittingly slip into a silo and still accomplish great things, but you limit your impact when you do not engage others in the work you are doing. Our silos allow us to remain in our comfort zone and work around only those who are most familiar. One of the most powerful stories in the Bible is the story of Mephibosheth (2 Samuel 9). He was dropped by a nurse at age five and, as a consequence, was crippled in both feet. Not only that, but he was the only remaining heir of King Saul, Israel's former king who had been killed in battle by David's army.

Mephibosheth ended up on the outskirts of Jerusalem in a place called Lodebar, a city that represented hopelessness and despair, similar to many of the places where we find people in need today. The underserved and marginalized areas are Lodebars. King David made a request for anyone who was left in the house of Saul to come forward, so he could show kindness. David was also in Jerusalem, and he had a vision to help and the resources to do so, but he had to get his vision to the person who needed it the most.

Here is where collaboration shows up. The king's servant indicated that Jonathan had a son, referring to Mephibosheth. After this revelation, the king's servant Ziba was instructed to leave the comfort of the king's palace in Jerusalem and go to Lodebar and get Mephibosheth. When he did, Mephibosheth was brought to Jerusalem and given a seat at the king's table. David didn't wait for Mephibosheth to come to him. David sent his messenger to Lodebar.

Collaboration will never be effective unless you are willing to go to Lodebar. It's when we are willing to roll up our sleeves and partner with others who are willing to go with us into places we have never been that we will see progress. There is a real need in Lodebar, and to put up an advertisement may not be sufficient. Sending Ziba represents our ability to go into spaces where we have traditionally been uncomfortable. You can't get the community engaged if you are not willing to commune with them first.

Who are the key stakeholders in the community? What are real needs? What things have worked well and what has not? All of these questions are answered when you go into Lodebar and seek to engage rather than throw vision "against the wall" and hope something will stick.

Collaboration requires us to look introspectively at how we have typically functioned and be willing to make adjustments. In an effort to become more collaborative, I overhauled the way our church staff was operating in order to foster a better working environment. This model was put in place in order to prevent miscommunication and to create more opportunities for shared input.

Historically, many church leaders operate out of a "big chief" motif. The leader envisions and implements vision, and others are simply given directives. There is no room for creative ideas or collective discussion. I felt this model was unhealthy, so I took a risk and decided to reconstruct a model that would allow us to be collaborative. I felt that if we were collaborative internally as a church staff, it would be easier to embrace it externally, because it would become part of our culture.

This shift was not easy for some. People get used to operating a certain way and holding on to power they assume they have. I learned to give space for people to embrace this transition, but I could not hold it back and miss our NOW moment.

Our organizational flow chart was like many others. It was hierarchical. It was top-down and reminded everyone who they reported to. Though that had its place, I believe that hierarchical models are not as effective as the relational model I was about to implement. I drew a circle on the board and put me in the middle. I took all my managers of specific areas and put them around the circle, representing a team approach rather than a chain-of-command approach.

All of our managers now meet twice a month to strategize. When I share vision, I share it with them and ask for and respect their input. They are encouraged to bring their team members into the meeting. I don't want to miss out on an idea that could potentially enhance the work we are attempting to do. We use the word *team* purposely, because we want staff persons to feel valuable and know that the organization values their input.

As a team, we share ideas and debate the best ways to implement the vision. The insight that they bring is phenomenal, and it is a better use of human capital. This model also limits scheduling conflicts and prevents us from having to reinvent the wheel. This model works because it is relational. When people feel they are in a controlled or forced environment, it becomes difficult to have maximum output. All my managers are now on the same level, and this system is proving effective, because in order for one area to be successful, it has to collaborate with another. Strategic partnership is what makes collaboration work.

THE RIGHT PARTNERSHIPS

You cannot achieve your destiny without the right partnerships. We must not confuse the need for partnership with being needy. Jesus demonstrated the need for partnership during the time of his earthly ministry. Jesus could have made it to His place of destiny alone, but He used wisdom in His pursuit. Jesus knew that He could make it to his destination sooner by having more people to provide help along the way. This helped to lessen the burden on any one individual or group. English writer John Heywood once stated, "Many hands make light work."[1] The more effective people you have on your team, the more work you can accomplish in less time.

Collaboration within any organization fosters innovation. Having the right people with you on your journey will allow for the collective thoughts to work together to accomplish a specific goal. For example, in Mark 2:1-5, the Gospel writer tells the story about the four men who worked collaboratively to get a paralytic man to Jesus:

---

1 https://en.wikipedia.org/wiki/John_Heywood; https://www.unrwa.org/sites/default/files/inspirational_teamwork_quotes_and_teamwork_quotations.pdf.

> And again he entered into Capernaum after some days; and it was noised that he was in the house. And straightway many were gathered together, insomuch that there was no room to receive them, no, not so much as about the door: and he preached the word unto them. And they come unto him, bringing one sick of the palsy, which was borne of four. And when they could not come nigh unto him for the press, they uncovered the roof where he was: and when they had broken it up, they let down the bed wherein the sick of the palsy lay. When Jesus saw their faith, he said unto the sick of the palsy, Son, thy sins be forgiven thee.

It wasn't the faith of the paralytic man alone that moved him from a state of needing help to being healed. It was the collaborative effort of others who joined together to carry the man to Jesus, coupled with their innovative idea to tear the roof off in order to get through the crowd to get to Jesus, that made their mission successful.

Don't delay your destiny attempting to do everything by yourself. You need the right people in your life to ensure you are able to make great things happen. If you are going to be successful, you have to make the right connections. This begins by surrounding yourself with people who are dedicated to their vocation.

When you look at the ministry of Jesus, He gives us insight into his strategy of collaboration. The people Jesus selected to be part of his ministry were busy in their own area of vocation when he found them. We saw in Matthew 4:18-22 how He called four of His disciples. Let's look further at Luke 6:12-16:

> Partner with "drivers."

> Now it came to pass in those days that He went out to the mountain to pray, and continued all night in prayer to God. And when it was day, He called His disciples to Himself; and from them He chose twelve whom He also named apostles: Simon, whom He also named Peter, and Andrew his brother; James and John; Philip and Bartholomew; Matthew and Thomas; James the son of Alphaeus, and Simon called the Zealot; Judas the son of James, and Judas Iscariot who also became a traitor.

Jesus invited those who were already doing something to partner with Him. If your people are doing nothing, they will continue to do nothing with you. I believe there are two kinds of people who want to connect with you. Drivers and passengers. Drivers grab hold to vision and push hard far beyond what is required, while passengers will sit and allow you to drive the vision. They do minimal work but want maximum benefit. You need drivers in your life. Your vision demands it.

When you are committed to collaboration, you seek partners who are passionate and creative. You cannot be a cutting-edge thinker and developer if your circle of people always depends on you to do all the thinking or even the best thinking in the room. Remember what Proverbs 27:17 declares: "As iron sharpens iron, so a man sharpens the countenance of his friend." As you are moving toward this next season, you need people in your life who are passionate about the things they are called to do and who have a high level of creativity.

Proverbs 8:12 (KJV) states that God will give you witty ideas and inventions: "I wisdom dwell with prudence, and find out knowledge of witty inventions." In order to position yourself to receive this God-given inspiration, surround yourself with people who also dwell in the space where they can conceive imaginative ideas and invent the things that have yet to be seen with the natural eye.

Famous playwright George Bernard Shaw once stated, "Some men see things as they are and say 'Why?' I dream of things that never were and say 'Why not?' " You need people around you who are okay with your "Why not?" questions and allow you to dream big, free of judgment.

These are characteristics of highly creative people.[2]

1. **Creative people display a great deal of curiosity about many things.** These people are constantly asking questions and tend to have a broad range of interest. They are often concerned with philosophical problems, for example, religion, values, the meaning of life.
2. **Creative people generate a large number of ideas or solutions to problems and questions.** These people are solution-oriented, they don't spend a great deal of time dwelling on a problem. They are fixers and want to move on to the next thing.
3. **Creative people are willing to take risks.** These individuals are labeled as adventurous or risk-takers.
4. **Creative people exhibits a good deal of intellectual playfulness**. These individuals have a vivid imagination, and they often daydream or wonder about things out loud.

---

2 http://thesecondprinciple.com/creativity/creativetraits/. Adapted from *The Second Principle* by Leslie Owen Wilson, Ed.D.

5. **Creative people have a great sense of humor.** These individuals often find comic relief in situations that others may not find funny.
6. **Creative people enjoy aesthetic impressions.** They exhibit a heightened sensitivity to beauty and are visibly moved by aesthetic experiences.
7. **Creative people typically do not conform**. These persons are not interested in details, are described as individualistic, and are comfortable with being labeled "different." Often, highly creative people are straightforward, forthright, and candid in dealing with others.

HOW TO MAKE DECISIONS

An important part of the collaborative process is how you make decisions. Your decisions affect the whole enterprise, so make them from a place of maturity. Paul gives his personal testimony of growing up and making mature decisions in 1 Corinthians 13:11: "When I was a child, I spoke as a child, I understood as a child, I thought as a child; but when I became a man, I put away childish things." Your ignorance or immaturity can only be excused for so long. Acts 17:30 declares, "Truly, these times of ignorance God overlooked, but now commands all men everywhere to repent."

At some point, you have to turn away from immature decisions and learn to make decisions that will produce long-term benefits. As you grow, develop, and mature as a leader, you cannot afford to make permanent decisions in temporary situations. As time goes on, your ability to make judgments concerning decisions will increase.

Paul says in 1 Corinthians 13:12, "For now we see in a mirror, dimly, but then face to face. Now I know in part, but then I shall know just as I also am known." If your decisions are not mature, they will erode the trust in the collaborative process of your team, thereby putting your vision at risk. If people working alongside us believe that they have to second-guess our ability in order to do what's in the best interest of the team, it will compromise your ability to get things done.

Mature decision-making involves learning how to be proactive rather than reactive. There comes a point in your life when you must learn to make wise decisions that go beyond your current situation. Your decision-making process must be strategic. This doesn't mean you have to become cold and calculating, but make sure that every move you make is one that will lead you in the direction of your destiny. Paul writes in Romans 8:5-8:

> For those who live according to the flesh set their minds on the things of the flesh, but those who live according to the Spirit, the things of the Spirit. For to be carnally minded is death, but to be spiritually minded is life and peace. Because the carnal mind is enmity against God; for it is not subject to the law of God, nor indeed can be. So then, those who are in the flesh cannot please God."

Those who live according to the flesh are reactive, because they are primarily focused on their feelings and what just happened and who did what to them. But those who live according to the Spirit are not reactive, they are proactive, because they already saw it coming in their spirit. When you live according to the Spirit, God will reveal to you what is up ahead. Luke says in

> Surely the Lord GOD does nothing, unless He reveals His secret to His servants the prophets.
> —Amos 3:7

8:17, "For nothing is secret that will not be revealed, nor anything hidden that will not be known and come to light."

When you learn how to position yourself in a place where you can hear from God, you will not be left in the dark concerning the things that are going on around you and what is next in your life. This does not mean that you can predict the future. Only God knows what's ahead. But it does mean that God will provide you with the revelation necessary to become a strategic planner of your life. You will have a greater sense of the strengths and weakness of those on your team. You will also have a greater sense of how and when to engage certain collaborative relationships.

MEASURE YOUR DELIVERABLES

When you bring people alongside the work you are doing, implement certain measurables. Can those in partnership with you move with you when you go to the next level? Can the people in your life properly relate to you on the next level? The larger question is, Can the people in your life transcend into every season with you? There are some people who can only be with you during your "right now." They are not cut out to handle your next move. And if they can't handle your next move, which is only a shift from your "right now," your leap to your "not yet" will really cause them to be disenchanted with your progress.

You need people connected with you who believe in what you are doing, who can stand in faith with you. Measurables give you milestones that your team can see. They help you mark your progress. They help show how bright your light is, because if your light is shining bright and theirs is not even lit, they will create darkness in the places where you are trying to bring light and revelation.

Being unequally yoked is so much more than addressing the issue of those who are saved being in relationship with the unsaved. You can be unequally yoked with people who are saved but who are not on the same emotional, intellectual, or spiritual level as you are. You need people in your life who can match you at every level of your life. When you move, they move; and when they move, you move. When you have people in your life who are equally yoked and walk in agreement with you, whatever you set out to accomplish, it will come to pass.

Again I say to you that if two of you agree on earth concerning anything that they ask, it will be done for them by My Father in heaven.

—Matthew 18:19

CONCLUSION

The right attitude as well as the right people are vital to the effectiveness of the collaborative process and a NOW culture. Jesus was strategic, and those who partnered with Him helped Him fulfill His mission in the earth.

Working solo in your silo is a model that puts serious limitations on your vision. Whatever you attempt to accomplish, pray for the right connections to people who understand where you are trying to go and who will join you in moving the needle of change and impact forward. In the words of Helen Keller, "Alone we can do so little; together we can do so much."[3] At the end of the day, remember that we are better together.

QUESTIONS

1. Are you a driver or a passenger? Why?
2. How has collaboration helped, or hurt, your vision?
3. How is "working in a silo" detrimental to the progress of your vision?
4. What does it mean to be "unequally yoked"? How would that harm God's purpose for your life?
5. How can you more effectively bring your resources to other people?

3 https://www.goodreads.com/quotes/tag/collaboration.

8

REMAIN RELEVANT

Now that you have a clear understanding of the importance of collaboration, we can now discuss relevance. One of the goals for surrounding yourself with the right people is that they will help you remain relevant.

Relevance is illusive for some people, because it causes them to stretch beyond tradition. Tradition is nothing more than frozen success. When you are seeking to remain relevant, you are committed to learning best practices in your field as well as having the courage to implement them. It takes courage, because introducing new ideas into older systems often creates tension. Sometimes you may have to restructure all together, but at a minimum redaction is required. Jesus understood this tension well when He said,

> No one pours new wine into old wineskins. Otherwise, the wine will burst the skins and both the wine and the wineskins will be ruined. No, they pour new wine into new wineskins. (Mark 2:22, NIV)

If you are going to execute vision, be sure that what you are offering is not based on assumptions purely from historical data.

Tradition is nothing more than frozen success.

Making assumptions based on the past has its place, but carefully base your analysis on current trends. I've shared with leaders around the world that you can't have an 8-track vision application in a virtual age. If a person has the most amazing music, but if it is on an antiquated 8-track tape, no modern car can play it. Technology has advanced such that it can no longer accommodate previous methodologies. There are a lot people who get stuck in a time warp trying to maintain relevance, but it won't happen unless you are willing to make some serious adaptations so that your vision can thrive.

BE A STUDENT OF CULTURE

In order to remain relevant, be a student of culture. You cannot isolate yourself from the things happening around you. Be willing to learn from what you affirm and what you vehemently don't. Life is the best teacher, and every day wake up with a heightened awareness, asking, *What will this day teach me?* Things change fast. Think about the last phone you purchased. At the time of your purchase, the next model was already in production. Technology is moving at a rapid pace.

The needs of people are changing as well. One of the things that saddens me is watching churches that were once thriving 20 years ago struggle to stay open today. What happened? For many, they felt that their way of doing things would transcend time and the successes they enjoyed in one generation would transfer to another one.

> Marry the vision, but date the method.
>
> —Bishop Paul Morton

Bishop Paul Morton said something incredibly profound concerning relevance: "Marry the vision, but date the method." What he meant is that the vision should not be compromised. It's what God gave you, so it is what it is. However, the method to deliver the vision should not have long-term status in our lives. We should be willing to change the methods in order that the vision can survive. Remember, you're not changing the gift; you are just changing the wrapping paper.

McDonald's does not change the Big Mac; they just change how they market it. When there is a new movie coming out, you might see a new advertisement associated with the purchase of a Big Mac, but the burger remains the same. The entire store can be decorated in Spiderman or Batman regalia, but the mainstays on the menu are constant. Relevancy is a delicate balance between continuity and change.

BE OPEN TO POSITIVE CHANGE

Executing vision requires you to be open to positive change. Everybody loves change until it personally affects them. Change challenges us. When our hair turns gray, we dye it black. When changes occur in our body due to age, we attempt to resist.

There is a saying in the church: "The things I used to do, I don't do anymore." I've discovered there is an amendment to that phrase. "The things you used to do, you *can't* do anymore."

Change brings out a level of anxiety within us. We struggle with issues of our personal significance in the midst of it. Questions begin to emerge. What do I do now? Am I included in the change? There is a level of stress associated with change. However, you can't resist the tension of change if your vision is going to remain relevant.

As the leader, if you expect change out of those connected to you, be the first person who is willing to go through a process of change. Leo Tolstoy once stated, "Everyone thinks of changing the world, but no one thinks of changing himself."[1] Others will be more inclined to change with you if they first see the change begin in you. Change may cause you to feel uncertain and even uncomfortable; but in order to move your vision forward, be willing to enter a season of change.

Your clothes enter the washing machine dirty, but through the process of friction and tension, they get clean. Embrace the tension if you want relevance, and prepare yourself for those who are close to you to question your decisions. As a leader, do what is necessary, because your decisions are not just for the present, they are for the future.

Considering the fact that friction and tension are parts of change, it should be clear that there is a cost to maintaining relevancy. Let's examine a biblical story to see how change and relevancy impacted the lives of others. When Jesus launched His

---

1 https://www.goodreads.com/author/quotes/128382.Leo_Tolstoy.

ministry, Matthew (4:16, KJV) says, "The people which sat in darkness saw great light; and to them which sat in the region and shadow of death light is sprung up." Then John says (1:5, NASB), "The Light shines in the darkness, and the darkness did not comprehend it." These two Scriptures give us an incredible insight into how people handle change.

Imagine sitting in a dark theater for an hour. Eventually, your pupils will expand, allowing the maximum amount of light in while you sit in the darkness. What this means is that you will begin to adjust to the darkness. You will know where your drink, popcorn, purse, and jacket are. Within the hour, darkness has become normative for light. If someone walks in from the noon sunlight and enters the dark theater where you are and trips over your foot, the first thing you think is, *What's wrong? Can't he see?* Because you've been in darkness so long, you have adjusted to it as your new normal.

Light is seen as an intrusion. Consequently, the darkness does not comprehend the light. When people sit in certain environments, they become accustomed to a particular ethos and praxis. They think, *That's the way it is for everybody. That's normal.* So when the need for change approaches, the immediate response is to reject it, because it is seen as a threat to what they have become accustomed to. This is why those who implement change must do it with a level of sensitivity and pace that allows those who are within the system to adjust to it.

You wouldn't take a flash light in to a movie theater and put it in the eyes of a person who has been in darkness for an hour. The same is true when implementing your vision for relevancy. Gradually recess the light or the knowledge so that they can receive it rather than reject it.

RESILIENCE

In your pursuit of relevancy, you also have to maintain a level of resilience. Those on the front line of relevancy will tell you that it does not happen without persecution and misunderstanding. Jesus was always misunderstood, particularly in regard to being in conflict with the law of Moses. Jesus gave clarity to this by stating in Matthew 5:17 (KJV), "Think not that I am come to destroy the law, or the prophets: I am not come to destroy, but to fulfil."

In essence, Jesus was saying that He had come to make the Law relevant in another generation. There is no compromising the spirit of the Law. Rather, it's important that a new generation is able to understand it and apply it to their lives.

Often, people are threatened by your attempts at relevancy, because they see it as a dismantling of what has been. I see many people who demonize and publicly speak negatively about systems to which they are attempting to bring relevancy. Honor what was so that you can leverage it to build the future. There cannot be destiny if you completely devalue your history. Relevancy occurs when you are able to salvage what's necessary, release what must go, and implement what is needed for a sustainable future. I've seen many leaders miss moments because of their inability to do this properly.

Dogs don't bark at parked cars.

Young pastors are called to churches and immediately begin implementing new ideas without understanding the time needed for those changes to be ingested and digested by the people. Needless to say, their tenure is tumultuous and, in some cases, short.

I've seen people full of ideas and passion get corporate jobs, but they didn't fully know how to engage the system so that their ideas would be received. There is a strategy involved when moving toward relevancy. Even when you do all the right things, you should still expect criticism.

Dogs don't bark at parked cars. Whenever you are moving and making changes, it will always attract adversity. Be determined to see it through. You cannot allow the negative forces to convince you it's not needed, because the future of the organization and the vision are at stake. Organizations don't just wake up extinct. Things end up that way because of neglect and fear of doing what is needed.

STAY CUTTING-EDGE

One of the things I've learned as a visionary is that I can never get comfortable if I am going to remain *cutting-edge*. I have to constantly read and study the newest trends so that I can stay on top of what's working. Church has changed over the last 20 years. The gospel has not, but church has.

When I was younger, people would stay in church two or three hours. There would be five-night revivals. People would come every week to Sunday school, church, and Bible study. Now, in a fast-paced world, people don't stay in church that long.

I'll share a funny story. I was asked to preach at a Presbyterian church a few years ago, and I asked repeatedly how long should I preach. They kept responding by telling me to take my time. I explained further my context and what I was accustomed to in some of the churches I had been invited to preach in. They told me to take as long as I wanted to, but they would be leaving at noon.

This story speaks to the fact that our vision must align itself with our intended audience. In our church, we've built an entire virtual ministry to remain relevant and meet the needs of those who are unable to attend physically or just don't want to attend. We started a Saturday service to accommodate those who work on Sundays, and we also have a commitment to keep our services at 1½ hours.

Part of my responsibility is not just to exegete Scripture to preach but also to exegete culture so that I can remain relevant. I am incredibly thankful that the Mount Zion Church of Nashville continues to thrive and remain relevant, but I also realize that in order for there to be sustainability, we must be eternal students.

BE FLEXIBLE. BE AWARE. BE YOUR OWN TOUGHEST CRITIC.

Your vision must be elastic enough to be flexible and to bend toward needs when they emerge. Never allow your vision to be so static or set in concrete that it operates within the confines of a self-made box. You need people around you who think outside the box.

Can you imagine what would have happened had the man who Jesus healed, the person whose friends lowered him through the roof, relied on traditional means to get a miracle? The men who carried him were so determined to get him the help he needed that they refused to allow the current state of affairs to determine the man's destiny. Some people would have said that the room is too crowded and there is no way in, but these men were willing to go through the roof. This is unconventional.

Relevancy is often birthed through unconventional means. When you are willing to do something that raises someone's eyebrow, you are moving in the right direction. The changes you see today may be out of date tomorrow. Relevance requires self-assessment and reflection. Be honest with yourself about where you are in order to maintain it, and be flexible enough to keep casting the vision.

A lot of leaders make the mistake of living in the successes of their past. It's like the people we all see at homecoming at our alma mater who have not gotten the memo that it's 20 years later. Don't allow nostalgia to make you a prisoner of your past accomplishments. The customer base you enjoyed in one generation may not be drawn to you in another, unless you are willing to do some serious overhaul. This demands flexibility. You can't allow pride to convince you that you are all right with how it's always been.

While in decline, I've heard many leaders lament that something is wrong with everything and everyone else other than themselves. If your vision is going to thrive, be your toughest critic. Be willing to deal with real numbers, not assumed ones; and deal with how your company, product, ministry, or vision is being perceived. Some people make the mistake of saying that people's perceptions don't matter, but they mattered to Jesus when He asked, "Who do men say that I am?"

Perception unchallenged becomes reality. You have to pay attention to how your organization is being perceived, because it can either propel you into your future or keep you locked into your past.

A WORD ABOUT NEEDS AND FEEDBACK

Leading a large church, I began to realize that some people wanted to feel more comfortable in smaller groups. By implanting this in our ministry, it met a need. Let me speak a word on needs. Whatever we do within the realm of purpose is ministry. Ministry does not only or even have to take place within the context of religious institutions. There is a ministry in the marketplace. You go to work or into your business space, and that's a space for ministry.

> People have too many options for you not to be concerned with their needs.

In order for ministry to be effective, it must meet a need. That's what ministry does. It meets needs. How can you actually meet the need if you aren't aware of what the need is? What our team realized is that it was important for us to survey the congregation to gather enough data so that we could steward ministry in the appropriate direction. You cannot create programs in a vacuum and expect people to support it because you and your team think it's a great idea. You and I are not in a position to assume what people's needs are. Be willing to ask the people what's working and what's not.

When you create an environment where honest feedback is welcome, you allow your organization space to grow. When people feel they have no input or that their opinions don't matter, they will simply disconnect from your organization or business and find one that meets their needs. According to Chip Heath and Dan Heath, "What looks like resistance is often a lack of clarity,"[2] which

---

2 Heath, C., & Heath, D. (2010). *Switch: How to Change Things When Change Is Hard.* New York: Broadway Books.

is why you must be intentional about including the people you serve in the changes you seek to implement. Otherwise, the things you seek to institute will be met with unnecessary opposition. People have too many options for you not to be concerned with their needs. Some of the feedback may be painful to hear. Some of it may challenge you as a leader, but never take it personally.

I've seen leaders make the mistake of ostracizing people who were honest. These actions sent shock waves through their organization and discouraged others from sharing their thoughts for fear of retaliation. What emerged was a culture of private pain and disillusionment.

You've probably been in meetings where the leader asked, "Are there any questions or comments?" and that deafening silence came over the room. These environments are unhealthy at best. Encourage people to be brutally honest, because you would rather have people who are invested in your vision tell you the truth than those who are not. Some of the most useful information I have ever gotten has not come from a book. It has come from a concerned and invested congregant who wanted to see things get better. When you label people complainers because their opinion differs from yours, you rob yourself of an opportunity to learn how your organization is being perceived as well as ideas that will assure it remains relevant.

Have you ever thought about the fact that the words *listen* and *silent* have the same letters? Perhaps if we as leaders and visionaries were a little more silent, we could hear what matters so that we can implement ministry and vision that meets the needs of the people who need it most.

Your vision is too important not to take relevancy seriously. I've often said that if a vision dies with the visionary, it wasn't a good vision. Vision must outlive you. Think of things five to ten years up the road. Your strategy cannot be just for today. Where do you see your organization or business in the future? Are your practices yielding positive results, or do they need redaction? These are just a few questions you have to ask yourself as you maintain relevancy.

I've often encouraged visionaries to surround themselves with people who are thinking about things that don't exist yet. There is a space in which people who are relevant live. It's in that "not yet" space that you are thinking about your next move. Some companies are making plans now for the future about how they staff. Television stations are making plans to be completely HD in a few years. Car manufacturers are planning to introduce more electric cars, because they see the future. Everything around you is preparing for what's to come.

Romans 8:22 (NIV) says, "We know that the whole creation has been groaning as in the pains of childbirth right up to the present time." Nobody waits until a child gets here to start planning the nursery; they do it in advance. If you are going to be relevant, learn to start making preparations NOW! That's what *No Opportunity Wasted* is all about. It's about not allowing these precious moments to pass you by. View relevancy as the lifeline of your vision. Relevancy is what keeps it breathing and functional. When you wake up in the morning, ask God to breathe new life on your vision so it never becomes stale.

BE AGILE

If you want to remain relevant, be willing to make adjustments on a dime. You never know what's around the corner. With all the things happening in the world, one day your business can be a dance studio for kids and the next week transformed into a shelter for those displaced in your city after a natural disaster. The apostle Paul's words in 1 Corinthians 9:19-23 (NIV) speak to this in a profound way.

> Though I am free and belong to no one, I have made myself a slave to everyone, to win as many as possible. To the Jews I became like a Jew, to win the Jews. To those under the law I became like one under the law (though I myself am not under the law), so as to win those under the law. To those not having the law I became like one not having the law (though I am not free from God's law but am under Christ's law), so as to win those not having the law. To the weak I became weak, to win the weak. I have become all things to all people so that by all possible means I might save some. I do all this for the sake of the gospel, that I may share in its blessings.

CONCLUSION

I am convinced that true visionaries will never allow their institutions to die. If you are reading this book, you have a commitment to do what is necessary for the preservation of your organization. Relevancy is not a respecter of persons. It places a demand among the struggling organization as well as the one that is thriving.

Every day you wake up, ask yourself and ask God how you can get better. Push yourself past yesterday's successes and embrace new challenges. Executing vision means you are completely engaged in the process and not a bystander. Be at the table with this work. As the visionary, listen attentively, study voraciously, and act courageously so that everything you hope to accomplish comes to pass.

QUESTIONS

1. How relevant are you personally and professionally?
2. How difficult is it for you to change?
3. Do you hire to your strengths? Are you intentional about creating new professional relationships?
4. How often are you intentional about networking with new people?
5. In what ways do you push past your yesterday?

9

STAY PREPARED

When you are in the midst of growing your business or organization, stay prepared so that you won't miss opportunities. Many people take for granted this process because they assume they have arrived. It is essential that you are constantly putting yourself in a position to learn.

God is so invested in your preparation that He providentially orchestrates experiences to assure that it will happen. Preparation is the key to more opportunities. When we fail to prepare, opportunities are wasted. Preparation meets opportunity. If you have a lack of opportunities in your life, it may be a result of a lack of or limited preparation.

Let's examine the importance of preparation. To begin, those who prepare live less stressful lives. I developed a system in my sermon preparation that allows me to prepare my sermons two months in advance. This creates room for me to give full attention

Proper planning prevents poor performance.

to the inevitable emergencies that will arise without affecting my study time. I'm never cramming my study time into the same week I preach. Planning my preaching frees up significant time to accomplish the other things that need to be done. This process requires me to spend at least three hours a day in my favorite coffee shop, but it pays huge dividends in terms of freeing up my time.

When you are attempting to manifest vision, how you prepare speaks to the value you place upon your assignment. Every experience should be seen as preparation for where God is taking you. There is a saying regarding preparation: "Proper planning prevents poor performance." Your pursuit of destiny requires a successful journey through the preparation process. There are no shortcuts through the preparation process. Take the time to be fully developed so you can be released into your place of destiny.

Before the age of digital photos, the best photos were developed in a darkroom. When something is developed in a darkroom, it is essential that there is no exposure to light, or else the picture will be ruined. Don't lose sight of the image God has shown you, because you are trying to reveal your destiny to others before you have been developed in the darkroom behind the scenes.

Proverbs 24:27 says, "Prepare your outside work, make it fit for yourself in the field; and afterward build your house." The Message Bible says it like this: "First plant your fields; then build your barn." First, plant the field before building the barn to store the harvest. We often become so overzealous in our pursuit of destiny that we forfeit the planting season and try to start building without proper preparation. No one fulfills their destiny that way. Without going through the preparation process of planning and planting, you are destined to end up with empty barns, empty buildings, and ultimately an empty destiny.

SEEK GOD FIRST

In order to prepare properly, you have to seek God first. Matthew 6:33 declares, "But seek first the kingdom of God and His righteousness, and all these things shall be added to you." God and God's ways must be first on your checklist of things to take place during your pursuit of destiny. When you seek God early on, there will be no need for retractions concerning your pursuit of destiny. Without first seeking God's guidance, you will keep having to redact and retract from your storyline regarding your pursuit of destiny, because you are moving forward without His counsel. Proverbs 19:21 says, "There are many plans in a man's heart, nevertheless the Lord's counsel—that will stand."

When you make plans, it is essential that you don't make them without prayer. Your prayer life should be a priority in the preparations process. You worry much less about what tomorrow or the future will bring if you pray about what you are seeking God to do in your life.

Planning is necessary, but you need to first pray and ask God to direct your

> Be anxious for nothing, but in everything by prayer and supplication, with thanksgiving, let your requests be made known to God.
>
> —Philippians 4:6

plans. Proverbs 16:3 declares, "Commit your works to the Lord, and your thoughts will be established." One of the things I've learned to do over the years is pray about everything. I don't accept invitations without prayer. I don't go into meetings or speak without prayer. I don't make purchases without prayer. Prayer keeps you in line with the will of God and prevents you from putting your vision in conflict. Pray about your current moves, and pray about your future moves.

SEPARATE YOURSELF

Another area of preparation is separation. Your willingness to separate yourself from the crowd will be necessary. When Jesus's destiny was realized through the start of his ministry, He immediately separated Himself from the crowd. Immediately following Jesus's baptism by John, and His confirmation as the Son of God, Jesus separated Himself as a method of preparation for his ministry.

Matthew 4:1 says, "Then Jesus was led up by the Spirit into the wilderness to be tempted by the devil." Jesus was led into the wilderness to fast and to pray, and it was also during this period of separation that He learned how to confront the devil and make him flee.

Separation from the crowd often allows you to tap into another level of strength, because during this time of replenishment, you open yourself to receive from the Spirit of God. The disciples continuously found Jesus stealing away from the crowd. In order to fully execute vision, take time to reset and to allow for uninterrupted time to commune with the Lord. This time allows you to make an assessment of your surroundings and weed out the unnecessary connections in your life. It's difficult to see the full picture if you are in the frame. Step outside of the frame so you can rest, reassess, and return refreshed.

Step outside of the frame so you can rest, reassess, and return refreshed.

Every job is a preparation. Every experience God gives you is designed for your development, not your destruction. Alice Walker once said, "Look closely at the present you are constructing, it should look like the future you are dreaming."[3] David is an excellent example of one who allowed every job to prepare him for destiny. While serving as a shepherd boy in his father's field, David developed his foundational skills of leadership that would prepare him for his destiny, to serve as the king of Israel. David gained the following on-the-job training skills:

1. David learned how to lead the sheep.
2. David learned how to feed the sheep.
3. David learned how to correct the sheep.
4. David learned how to protect the sheep.

What proved to be the turning point in his pursuit of destiny, David faced Goliath. When it was time for him to defeat the giant Goliath in the battle, David recalled his experience as a shepherd boy to prove his readiness for this moment.

---

3 https://www.goodreads.com/quotes/266067-look-closely-at-the-present-you-are-constructing-it-should.

> And Saul said to David, "You are not able to go against this Philistine to fight with him; for you are a youth, and he a man of war from his youth." But David said to Saul, "Your servant used to keep his father's sheep, and when a lion or a bear came and took a lamb out of the flock, I went out after it and struck it, and delivered the lamb from its mouth; and when it arose against me, I caught it by its beard, and struck and killed it. Your servant has killed both lion and bear; and this uncircumcised Philistine will be like one of them, seeing he has defied the armies of the living God." Moreover David said, "The LORD, who delivered me from the paw of the lion and from the paw of the bear, He will deliver me from the hand of this Philistine." And Saul said to David, "Go, and the LORD be with you!" (1 Samuel 17:33-37).

I was being prepared for where I am now long before I realized it. I worked with my father in his janitorial company as a young man. Working ten hours a day developed a strong work ethic in me. Watching my father clean windows and wax floors with so much dignity and excellence provided a lot of perspective for me. Every job we did, we finished on schedule and beyond what was expected. This was drilled into my spirit early as a young man, and now it is one of the guiding principles of everything I do. Going to work with my father in that white truck every morning during the summers helped craft the man I am today and pushed me to another level of work excellence. Get every lesson on every job you have, whether you enjoy the work or not. It's preparing something in you for where you are going.

SEEK THE EXTRAORDINARY

One of the lessons I share frequently with those I mentor is that they should never settle for the ordinary but always seek the extraordinary. You are not being prepared to be average. Average is simply being on top of the bottom. If you are going to do big things, prepare yourself accordingly.

Peter walking on the water is an example of a person who did not settle for ordinary experiences on the road to destiny. Peter had to be corrected on quite a few things, but one thing he can be commended for is his ability to seek the extraordinary. In Matthew 14:28-29, we find Peter defying gravity and walking on water.

> And Peter answered Him and said, "Lord, if it is You, command me to come to You on the water." So He said, "Come." And when Peter had come down out of the boat, he walked on the water to go to Jesus.

When you are in pursuit of destiny and serious about executing vision, the ordinary will be viewed as mundane, and only extraordinary experiences will satisfy you. Peter refused to remain in the confines of the boat. He chose to become a water-walker. When you are a water-walker, you are comfortable doing what others only dream about. This was Peter NOW moment, and he embraced it by stepping out. We can say what we want about Peter and his personal missteps, but what cannot be denied is that he did something nobody in history has ever done. He walked with Jesus on the water.

When you are serious about preparation, you make a commitment to sharpen your skills. The great boxing legend Muhammad Ali once stated,

> ions aren't made in gyms. Champions are rom something they have deep inside them —a desire, a dream, a vision. They have to have the skill, and the will. But the will must be stronger than the skill.[4]

KNOW YOURSELF

Preparation forces you to invest in yourself. In order to invest in yourself, spend time getting to know yourself. Investors take time getting to know the product in order be strategic in how much time and resources are necessary to yield the greatest amount of profit on their investment. Likewise, if you are going to invest in yourself, you need to conduct a case study on yourself. Ask yourself the following questions:

1. What are my most productive hours of the day?
2. What are my defined areas of skills and expertise?
3. What are my priorities in life?
4. How prepared am I for the opportunities I am seeking?
5. Am I aligned with the right people to reach my destiny?
6. Do I take advantages of opportunities that come my way?

In order to sharpen your skills and be successful at executing vision, develop a mindset that focuses on success. In order to create a successful mindset, there are several practices in which you should engage to ensure your mindset is that of one who is

---

4 http://masbenlifetalk.com/how-to-be-prepared-for-your-destiny-or-your-opportunities/.

destined to achieve greatness. Here are a few ways you can help create a successful mindset:

1. **Believe you will achieve what you have been called to accomplish.** Philippians 1:6 says, "Being confident of this very thing, that He who has begun a good work in you will complete it until the day of Jesus Christ." Remind yourself daily that there is something powerful at work in your life. God thought enough of you to make an investment, and your life must yield a return. There can be no room for doubt. If God allowed you to get into the program or the position, believe He placed within you the skills to achieve at a high level.
2. **Have a clear vision of your destiny.** The prophet Habakkuk (2:2) records the following words of the Lord: "Then the LORD answered me and said: 'Write the vision and make it plain on tablets, that he may run who reads it.'" If you don't have a clear understanding of where you are going, nobody else will. Bring your vision into greater focus by making the necessary adjustments. Your vision is too important to be a blur. People must be able to clearly delineate your vision and get excited about helping you move toward execution.
3. **Become a voracious reader.** When you are a voracious reader, you have an insatiable or unquenchable appetite for knowledge. Former president Harry S. Truman said, "Not all readers are leaders, but all leaders are readers." When you read and stay informed about a vast variety of topics and subject areas, you will develop the mindset of a successful person. The more knowledgeable you are, the more power you will possess. Proverbs 15:14 says, "The heart of him who has understanding seeks knowledge, but the mouth of fools

feeds on foolishness." One of the things that has been helpful for me is to read material from a variety of disciplines. Don't limit yourself to books in your field. I've discovered principles in other disciplines that have proven to be effective in mine.

4. **Be open to a higher level of thinking.** Your thoughts are finite, but the thoughts God has concerning you are infinite. Do not let your way of thinking limit you as you prepare for where God is taking you. God wants to blow your mind, but you have to be ready to entertain thinking that transcends what you can see with the natural eye. First Corinthians 2:9 says, "Eye has not seen, nor ear heard, nor have entered into the heart of man the things which God has prepared for those who love Him."

THE VALUE OF CONSISTENCY

As you go through the preparation process, consistency is key to your success. When you are serious about executing at higher levels, learn to be consistent. Without consistency, you will lack the ethic necessary to maintain the level of work required to operate on the next level. If you are not able to keep a job when you are an entry-level employee, how will you be trusted with an executive-level position?

The Scripture reminds us in 1 Corinthians 15:58, "Therefore, my beloved brethren, be steadfast, immovable, always abounding in the work of the Lord, knowing that your labor is not in vain in the Lord." Many people get frustrated because you are asked to do more than others who were hired to do the same job as you; but be mindful that you are not tasked with extra to remain at your current level. The extra that is required of you in this season is preparing you for your future.

I've come to understand that preparation put you on a path for the manifestation of your vision. As you pursue your dream, remember these 5 Ps during the process:

1. **Preparation.** There must be a period of preparation. Whatever God allows, embrace it as part of your preparation. The curriculum is set by God. He strategically prepares you for where He is taking you.

2. **Position.** Your period of preparation will get you in the right position. The opportunities ahead of you are being prepared during your preparation. The position or place that God has for you will be in alignment with your preparation. If it appears to be taking longer, it's because God is rearranging things with the position and setting other things in place so that when you arrive, everything will be in order. He will not allow you to prepare and release you into a negative situation. The position will be right for you.

3. **Productivity.** Once you are in the right position you will start to be productive. Everything that has been poured into you will begin to manifest when you are where God wants you to be. You will produce at a high level because you are in a place where your gifts and skills can flourish. Your ability to execute vision will catch the attention of others around you, because you are operating in your proverbial "sweet spot."

4. **Persecution.** Your productivity will attract adversity. I say often that dogs don't bark at parked cars. Your productivity will expose the insecurities of people around you. This season

of persecution is designed to discourage you from producing results. Instead, use it as confirmation that you are exactly where you need to be. Don't allow persecution to stifle your execution. Remember, you've been prepared for this.

5. **Promotion.** Your ability to endure the persecution you encounter on the way to destiny will lead you to a place of promotion. God does not promote because of tenure. He promotes because we pass tests. Your resilience and faithfulness are what set you up for promotion. Often, people will see you in a promoted state but have no idea of what it cost you.

The psalmist David, king of Israel, went through the process of being prepared, being placed in position, and becoming extremely productive, which led to his persecution. But because he was able to endure the season of persecution, he and his family received the promotion that was promised for his life.

This season will not be without trials and hardships, but even when the enemy sends attacks during your preparation season, it will teach you how to develop strategies to conquer the enemy on a higher level. Romans 8:18 (KJV) gives us this word of encouragement and assurance concerning the challenges you will face on your way to destiny: "For I reckon that the sufferings of this present time are not worthy to be compared with the glory which shall be revealed in us."

What's ahead of you is much greater than where you have been. If you learn to endure your time of suffering, your ability to deal with opposition will lead to moments of opportunity. Allow everything that you encounter during the process of preparation, the good and the bad, to help propel you into your destined place.

QUESTIONS

1. When has the lack of planning derailed your vision?
2. How has proper planning moved you forward in implementing your vision?
3. Consider King David's life and how his experiences prepared him for position. How have your experiences prepared you for what God has planned for you?
4. Ask yourself the questions in the section "Know Yourself." Were you surprised by your answers? How will this information help you to be better prepared for what's ahead?
5. Have you identified a personal or professional accountability partner?

10

FOCUS: KEEP YOUR EYES ON THE PRIZE

Like me, if you are constantly moving, maintaining focus is a constant challenge. I've often been told that once one thing is accomplished, I'm on to the next. Focus is something that requires a great deal of discipline. If your vision is going to come to pass, it requires great attention to detail and an unrelenting commitment to keep your eye on the prize.

There is a place called "origination," and then there is place called "destination." One is where we begin pursuing the vision; the other is where we manifest it. Between the two are a variety of things that have the capacity to take our attention in a direction contrary to the goal. If you are going to accomplish the goal you have set for yourself, master the art of discipline.

The ability to maintain focus is connected to the ability for you to be successful in your pursuits. If a ball player takes his eyes off the target, he'll miss his throw. Your productivity is a direct reflection of your priorities. When you possess the ability to concentrate solely on the task at hand, your success rate increases. Keep your eye on the big goals of your vision. Paulo Coelho, author of the book *The Alchemist*, states,

> You will keep him in perfect peace, whose mind is stayed on You, because he trusts in You.
>
> —Isaiah 26:3

"Whenever you want to achieve something, keep your eyes open, concentrate and make sure you know exactly what it is you want. No one can hit their target with their eyes closed."

One way the Bible describes sin is "missing the mark." To avoid missing the mark concerning your destiny, remain focused. With each intentional step forward, you get closer to your destiny. The key to maintaining focus is to remain focused on God. Colossians 3:2 instructs us to "set your mind on things above, not on things on the earth." Once you have a heavenly perspective, God will be able to lead and guide you to help direct your focus. Psalm 32:8 declares, "I will instruct you and teach you in the way you should go; I will guide you with My eye."

LIMIT DISTRACTIONS

In order to maintain focus, limit the distractions in your life. In a world with so many attractions, it is difficult to live a life free of distractions. But in order to become a focused person, be intentional in limiting the distractions in your life.

A good start is creating a place and time where you will not be disturbed. There should be certain times and spaces that are deemed sacred to you. In order to maintain focus, there have to be times in your life where you can have solace and become one with God. It is in these moments that you can regain a state of peace.

Don't crowd God out, allowing every moment to be filled with an activity, work, social media surfing, and other things that demand your attention. Learn to steal away from the crowd or the crowded lifestyle and allow yourself to regain focus. As you read this, you are probably wondering how that works with all the deadlines and meetings you have. But be intentional about carving out this time, so you can develop greater focus on the vision God has given to you.

Another step in increasing your focus is getting rid of the clutter in your life. In other words, learn how to clean up your life. Your physical, mental, and emotional spaces must be free in order for you to be focused on the things you have been assigned to accomplish. Dr. Eva Selhub says, "At the end of the day, being organized is about having more time for yourself, and enabling you to live a more balanced life.[1] . . . Clutter is stressful for the brain,

---

1 Eva Selhub, M.D., *Your Health Destiny: How to Unlock Your Natural Ability to Overcome Illness, Feel Better, and Live Longer.* http://www.shape.com/lifestyle/mind-and-body/how-cleaning-and-organizing-can-improve-your-physical-and-mental-health.

so you're more likely to resort to coping mechanisms such as choosing comfort foods or overeating than if you spend time in neater surroundings."[2]

You might have mental, spiritual, and emotional clutter, with built-up issues that have been hanging out in your life for years. It is time to serve your clutter an eviction notice and move forward with living a clutter-free life so that you can be focused on the days ahead.

Imagine your cell phone running out of space. When this happens, it is as a result of having too many applications and data on your phone. Often, you are unable to download new applications because there is no available space. You will have to delete old applications or purchase more space.

God may be saying to you, "I want to download new things into your life, but I can't until you delete some things that are occupying the space." What are you willing to let go of to get God's best? Clutter is more than having a junky house, car, or office. Clutter can be a result of your unwillingness to be free of familiar people and things that you have held on to for many years. It can also result in you having such deep attachment to these people, places, and things that your focus is limited and cannot expand to encompass all that God has in store for your destiny. In Mark 10: 17-22, we learn of the interaction between Jesus and the rich young ruler.

> Now as He was going out on the road, one came running, knelt before Him, and asked Him, "Good Teacher, what shall I do that I may inherit eternal life?" So Jesus said to him, "Why do you call Me good? No one is

2 Ibid.

> good but One, that is, God. You know the commandments: 'Do not commit adultery,' 'Do not murder,' 'Do not steal,' 'Do not bear false witness,' 'Do not defraud,' 'Honor your father and your mother.'" And he answered and said to Him, "Teacher, all these things I have kept from my youth." Then Jesus, looking at him, loved him, and said to him, "One thing you lack: Go your way, sell whatever you have and give to the poor, and you will have treasure in heaven; and come, take up the cross, and follow Me." But he was sad at this word, and went away sorrowful, for he had great possessions.

You can't be the master of your life if you are a slave to your time.

The ruler had a life filled with the world's riches, which is not a bad thing in and of itself. But when those things are so important that they crowd out time with Jesus, the world's riches have become part of the clutter that you need to be freed from in order to be focused on your relationship with God.

LIVING WITH SCHEDULES

Have you ever considered how focused your life would be if you learned how to live on a schedule? Everything in my life is done on schedule. Zig Ziglar said, "Lack of direction, not lack of time, is the problem. We all have twenty-four hour days."[3] We all have been given 24 hours a day, and we can choose to use them effectively or squander them. Beware of time thieves (people and things that

---

3 https://www.goodreads.com/quotes/tag/focus.

rob you of your time). Living by a schedule is not insensitive or unnatural. Scheduling every meeting and appointment will allow you to remain in control of your life. You can't be the master of your life if you are a slave to your time.

Create a to-do list, but also allow other people to put their "do" on your list. The reason why some people are always late to appointments is because they allow others to occupy time previously allocated. Focus is about staying on schedule so that you can remain productive.

I fly from Nashville to Atlanta often. The flight is actually 33 minutes, but they schedule it for 1 hour gate to gate. The rationale is that they have factored in the time it takes to get to the runway and the time it takes to get to the gate in the other city. By allowing this cushion, they remain on schedule.

If you are the person who has a meeting at 8:00 and you live 30 minutes away and decide to leave the house at 7:30, you are not as focused as you should be. Chances are you are often late to everything. Factor in what could happen, so that you give yourself enough time to adjust and still make your schedule.

When you take time seriously, you are committed to the goal. You will never get time back. It's unredeemable, so use it wisely and schedule things in a way that allows you to accomplish your goals rather than the goals of everyone else. Because time is something that you cannot get back, stewardship of time is essential. Not only do you have to learn how to value your time, you must learn to teach others around you how to respect your time. Here are a few things to remember concerning being a good steward of your time:

1. **Don't allow people to put themselves on your schedule without your permission.** When your time is limited, people should only be allowed to schedule time you have available for meetings. People have to be trained to respect the "appointment only" requirement for your time. The "walk-in" method does not work for those with busy schedules.
2. **Always have an agenda for a meeting.** Going into a meeting that you are leading without an agenda creates chaos. Having an agenda does not stifle creativity; it actually encourages creativity, because clear direction of the meeting expectations will eliminate wasted time going over things that may be irrelevant to the particular meeting.
3. **Be brief. Be brilliant. Be gone.**[4] Learn how to get your message across without taking all day to do it. Learn the beauty of brevity and move on to the next task.

Ephesians 5:15-17 (ESV) teaches us a lesson about time management.

> Look carefully then how you walk, not as unwise but as wise, making the best use of the time, because the days are evil. Therefore do not be foolish, but understand what the will of the Lord is.

Don't let the needs of others dictate your schedule. Their emergency is not your emergency. Make the most of your time each day to ensure your time and your vision's time are not wasted.

---

4 http://www.greatleadershipbydan.com/2010/11/leadership-off-wall.html.

> Let your eyes look straight ahead, and your eyelids look right before you.
> —Proverbs 4:25

SCHEDULE REFUELING STATIONS

There is no way to execute vision efficiently and effectively unless you have set aside time to refuel. Taking time to replenish helps you to maintain focus, because it allows you to get refueled along the journey. Take time to refuel your passion. If you do not make stops to fill up your car, at some point you will run out of gas. Nobody fills up a car with gas while it is in motion. You have to pull over, stop, and fill up. No matter how anxious you are about getting to your destination, gas stops are important if you are to make it. In Psalm 23:2-3, the psalmist declares the following about the refueling God brings into our lives:

> He makes me to lie down in green pastures; He leads me beside the still waters. He restores my soul; He leads me in the paths of righteousness for His name's sake.

Many people are not as focused as they should be, because they are drained from the journey. It's okay to pull over and fill up so you can reach your goal on all cylinders.

LET YOUR LIGHT SHINE

When you are focused, you don't lose sight of the main objective of your assignment. Physics teaches us that "without light, there would be no sight." The visual ability of humans and other animals is the result of the complex interaction with light, eyes, and the brain. We are able to see, because light from an object moves through space and reaches our eyes. Once light reaches our eyes, signals are sent to our brain, and our brain deciphers the information in order to detect the appearance, location, and movement of the objects we perceived. The whole process, as complex as it is, would not be possible if it were not for the presence of light.[5] This is known as light to sight.

Light to sight teaches us how light is necessary for sight, but *line of sight* teaches a little more about how light affects us. Line of sight, according to physics, states, "Everything that can be seen is seen only when light from that object travels to our eyes."[6] The bottom line of the line of sight principle is, "In order to view an object, you must align your sight in line with an object; and when you do, light will come from that object to your eye along the line of sight."[7]

The spiritual application regarding the line of sight is that if there is no Light (Jesus) in your situation, then you have no sight. John 8:12 records these words of Jesus: "Then Jesus spoke to them again, saying, 'I am the light of the world. He who follows Me shall not walk in darkness, but have the light of life.'" When Peter walked on the water, his mistake was losing his line of sight. If he had kept his eyes on Jesus, he never would have fallen in the water and began to sink.

When your vision is from God, then your line of sight remains on Him regardless of the distractions along the way. There will be

---

5 http://www.physicsclassroom.com/Class/refln/u13l1a.cfm.

6 http://www.physicsclassroom.com/class/refln/Lesson-1/The-Line-of-Sight.

7 Ibid.

no shortage of challenges that seek your full attention, but if you see God in the goal, your focus will be aimed in the direction of your destination, not your demise.

WHERE THERE IS LIGHT, THERE IS HOPE

You can live a life of expectancy when you consistently focus on your goal. It is difficult to focus on where God is taking you if you have little or no hope. Never allow adversity to push you past your hope. It doesn't matter what happens in your life, if you have a pulse, there is possibility, so keep moving forward.

METHODS TO HELP YOU LIVE FORWARD

- **Be excited for your future.** Don't depend on others to be excited for you concerning your future. God gave the vision to you, so you are responsible for fueling the flames of your passion on your way to your destined place. If someone stood in a crowded theater and said they had a check for $100,000 with your name on it, you would make a bee-line in their direction to receive it. You wouldn't be concerned with the opinions or looks people gave you. All that would matter would be the goal of getting the check. When you focus on the things people are saying about you and how they treat you, you have lost sight of the goal. Think about the awesome thing God is going to do in your life, and get excited about that. Don't waste energy responding to what people do to you, or else you'll lose focus on what God is doing for you. The prophet Jeremiah gives these words of hope concerning the future plans God has for you: "For I know the thoughts that I think toward you, says the LORD, thoughts of peace and not of evil, to give you a future and a hope" (Jeremiah 29:11).

- **Position yourself to move forward.** If you were to keep your car in the reverse gear, you would only go backward, returning to the destination where you were before. In order to move from where you have been to where you desire to go, put your car in drive and move forward. Think about how God made you. Your body is designed physiologically to go forward. If a person walks backward all the time, it's unnatural. If God wanted you to focus on the rear, he would have put an eyeball in the back of your head. Your eyes are in front for a reason. Keep moving forward. Don't rehearse the nightmare of your past and miss the destiny-filled dream in your future. Isaiah 43:18-19 says, "Do not remember the former things, nor consider the things of old. Behold, I will do a new thing, now it shall spring forth; Shall you not know it? I will even make a road in the wilderness and rivers in the desert." If you are going to spring forward, you can't cling to the past.
- **Learn to pause and rest.** Matthew 11: 28-30 encourages us to take rest from all of our heavy burdens: "Come to Me, all you who labor and are heavy laden, and I will give you rest. Take My yoke upon you and learn from Me, for I am gentle and lowly in heart, and you will find rest for your souls. For My yoke is easy and My burden is light." There is a feature on the Apple watch that will instruct you to breathe every so often each day. To some, this notification can be a nuisance, but most people will admit that we often move so fast throughout our day that we do not take the time to take a deep breath, pause, and rest from whatever is pulling on our

time and focus. This is an area where I needed a lot of help. I could not turn my phone off and go to bed. I would sleep with my phone next to me, because I felt it was important that I was accessible in case of an emergency at church. Needless to say, this prevented me from getting the necessary rest I needed. God convicted me and said that I didn't trust Him. He reminded me that He didn't need me to micromanage Him, because He would take care of things while I slept. Your God-given vision is in God's hands. Trust Him to cover it, and get the rest you need.

Throughout His life, Jesus maintained focus on His assignment in pursuit of destiny.

- At the young age of 12, Jesus was found at the Temple because He was focused on His destiny. In Luke 2:49, with laser-sharp focus, He responds to His parents' inquiry as to why He had remained behind in the Temple, causing them worry, by stating, "Why did you seek Me? Did you not know that I must be about My Father's business?"
- At age 30, when He was baptized before starting His ministry, Jesus immediately limited his distractions and had focused time with God during His 40-day wilderness experience.
- At age 33, even with impending death looming before him, Jesus maintained focus from Gethsemane to Calvary. Although he was in great pain and agony, He maintained focus on His assignment and the fulfillment of His destiny. Luke 22:42 tells us that Jesus said, "Father, if it is Your will, take this cup away from Me; nevertheless not My will, but Yours, be done."

- While Jesus was on the cross, He maintained focus with each of His seven sayings. He was taking care of business while dying on the cross at Calvary. Jesus never lost His focus and therefore fulfilled His assignment and made it to His place of destiny. Hebrews 8:1 declares, "Now this is the main point of the things we are saying: We have such a High Priest, who is seated at the right hand of the throne of the Majesty in the heavens." Jesus' main objective was to take on the sins of the world by dying on the cross, so that we could be in relationship with the Father. Jesus' place of destiny is on the right hand of the Father, where He makes daily intercession for us to remain in connection with the Father.

Maintaining focus like Jesus will ensure that we also make it to our place of destiny. Keep your eye on the prize. I assure you it's closer than it's ever been before.

QUESTIONS

1. What distracts you and causes you to lose your focus? How do you get back on track?
2. How does clutter affect you? What clutter would you need to get rid of in order to keep your focus where it needs to be?
3. How does Isaiah 26:3 speak to your ability to focus on God and His purpose for you?
4. Describe any struggles you have with time management. How can you improve how you manage your time?
5. How often do you remind yourself of your vision?

11

MAKE THE VISION WORK

By now, your vision is clear and up and running and you're not missing opportunities. That being said, I can assume based on my experiences with manifesting and executing vision, there are still challenges in getting things to work as you envisioned. Once vision is placed in other peoples' hands, it can be stifled; misunderstood; or, worse yet, considered dead on arrival.

I included this chapter because I wanted to share with you some reasons why vision fails. I want to show you how to get people engaged and explain some of the complications you may be experiencing with those you've entrusted with the vision. Vision means nothing if it does not work. As I said in the beginning, this book is not about theory, it's about practice. It's about execution.

One of the most difficult challenges you will face when executing vision is integrating others into your vision who were not there at the beginning. In order for your vision to remain fresh, allow space for new ideas and concepts to be shared. For many leaders, what they thought would be an easy integration was a difficult reality.

SYSTEM THINKING

Imagine your ministry or business as a system. There are inputs who engage your system. If your system is going to be effective, be willing to welcome all who desire to engage it. People engage your system under the assumption that something transformative will occur. The output must look different than the input if the system is going to be successful.

When you put dirty dishes in a dishwasher, there is an expectation that when you take them out they will be clean. If the dishes, pots, and pans come out the same way they went in, you've got a system failure. The same is true with your ministry or business. When you experience a system failure, do a proper analysis to get to the bottom of the problem.

For those of us who work in ministry, we operate under the scriptural mandate "Whosoever will, let them come." We don't place restrictions on who engages our system. But if there is no transformation in the lives of those who connect with us, we cannot put the blame on the input. If we are going to properly execute vision and make it work, we have to look at what may be happening within our system that prevents the desired results.

We now know there are inputs and outputs, but there are gatekeepers as well. Every system has those who have been entrusted by the visionary to protect the integrity of the vision.

Often these are your managers or your leaders. From what I've seen, much of the conflict within the systems occurs here.

For example, imagine a pastor meeting a man who just moved to the city and is the director of marketing for the state. He was highly recruited. He meets the pastor at a function, and the pastor invites the man to visit the church. The pastor is also thinking that this incredibly resourceful person could be a huge resource in expanding the church's marketing ministry.

The man visits the church and enjoys his experience there. After service, the pastor introduces him to the members of the marketing team in hopes that they will embrace him and integrate him into the system so that everyone can benefit from his wealth of knowledge. Rather than embrace the person, however, the marketing team offers only a lukewarm welcome. The director of marketing is given only menial tasks, because many on the team feel threatened by his presence. Rather than use and maximize this person's gifts, the team minimizes them. Now the man who was previously excited about the church loses interest and casually attends until he stops coming all together.

Does this sound familiar to you? I'm sure it does. It happens in every system. When people to whom you have entrusted to expand and integrate your vision become intimidated by greatness, they stop being gatekeepers and become vision-killers instead. I have seen this happen more than enough times, and often the visionary is unaware of what is happening.

Gatekeepers will speak on behalf of the leader, and their words will often misrepresent the heart of the leader. You would be amazed at the casualties that have engaged your system and have left bruised and broken. This is why you have to be careful who you allow to be the gatekeepers of your vision.

I would like to suggest a few things for your consideration. First, never make people gatekeepers if they have low self-esteem. When you do, you are setting them up for failure and putting your system in jeopardy. People who have low self-esteem allow their positions to define them and often cannot function without titles or authority. Then when persons show up with more experience or better qualifications, the gatekeepers go into *self-preservation* mode rather than in integration mode. They don't see brilliance around them as a compliment; they see it as competition. I have learned to give positions to people who don't need them.

One red flag you should pay attention to is when people engage your system solely because of their position rather than for relational purposes. What that suggests is that once their title or position changes, they no longer feel connected to the vision. When leaders appoint people to positions based on their need, they are literally passing out self-esteem. This puts a strain on the system and on the leader, because when changes are needed, the impact on the person who has been appointed can have consequences beyond the position. It can lead to depression, disillusionment, and even death. Don't put yourself in a situation where you fear moving someone because of what could happen if they no longer have their position.

Second, I would never make someone a gatekeeper who doesn't understand submission. People like this often are authoritative and exert power in your absence toward others under the guise that it was sanctioned by you. This is problematic because these people are often redacting your vision to fit their agendas. You would be amazed at the number of people who believe you said things you never did.

INTENTIONALLY DEVELOP YOUR TEAM

Intentionally develop your team, or system failure will result and prevent your vision from manifesting. Often, our systems are filled with toxic people who threaten everything we've worked hard for. If you allow toxic people to remain in your system, they will contaminate others within the system. The most vulnerable will be new people to the system, but no one is off limits.

I've seen toxic people develop their own disciples in the midst of systems. They develop a vision within the vision. Toxic people will contaminate your system and cause others to question your leadership.

I want to offer a few more things that can be helpful for you to make your system work. As discussed earlier, it's important to choose and assign your gatekeepers wisely. There must be an intentional effort focused on relationships. If your vision is going to manifest, shift toward a more relational atmosphere. If your system is going to have sustainability, you need to create ways to cultivate a culture of positive relationships. When you don't have a great relationship culture, you miss opportunities. Nobody wants to be around mean, territorial, or insecure people. Make certain that you are intentional about developing those you entrust with your vision, making sure they have your spirit.

What I have attempted to do as a leader is be more relational. Often, leaders are insulated within the system, and people rarely get to engage them. I have used a series of methods to deconstruct those assumptions and provide some direct access to me. I purposely use social media; I shake hands with people after every service; and I still do the work every day that reaches people where they are.

The reason the television show *Undercover Boss* is so powerful is because it gives CEOs an inside view of what their systems look like. Without relying solely on what managers tell them, they go undercover and establish direct relationships with employees to get honest feedback, which proves to be valuable in moving their companies to the next level.

The day of distant, *hard-to-reach* leaders is over. If you are going to be successful as a leader with a clear vision, be a relational leader. Leaderships set the pace and culture of the system. If you are highly relational, chances are those who work around you are that way as well.

TAKING RISKS

My next suggestion to make your system work is don't be afraid to take risks. I interpret Hebrews 11: 1 this way: "Now risk is the substance of things hoped for and the evidence of things not seen." Making things work often means you are required to take risks. But the risks you take are not random. They are calculated decisions that you deem necessary to the functionality of your system. When a leader takes risks, they usually do so understanding there will be backlash.

Early on, I took serious risks as a leader. I went on the college campuses and invested in and personally invited students to our church. When the church was small, people told me that it was not a good move to build a church focused on college students. They told me that college students are transient; they graduate and move on. But I kept taking risks by sending buses to the campuses to pick them up, providing free meals after service, and developing campus leaders who would represent our ministry at their respective campuses. I experienced criticism from people who didn't understand this investment and attack from others. However, this risk yielded incredible dividends.

Today, the Mount Zion Church has a college ministry that reaches thousands of students each year and has touched the lives of over 50,000 students since we began. If I had never taken those risks, we would have missed an incredible opportunity to touch the lives of so many young people. Our church now has a demographic that consists of around 45 percent millennials, while many others are struggling to reach this group. They are coming because we have created, within the system, a culture of relationship; and we took a risk by investing in them when others would not.

You are not bound by your cultural or ethnic context.

What risks are you contemplating? If you are going to make your system work, trust your instinct and take the risk so that your system will function and produce the desired results. But beware. Risks are often controversial, but they are necessary if you are going to have a system where things work.

RISK YIELDS GREATER REACH

When you take risks, the next thing that your system will experience is greater reach. The reason the director of marketing for the state, mentioned above, was not welcomed was because the system he was attempting to engage lacked the capacity to accommodate the gift he brought.

Imagine the people he could have brought with him into the system. Imagine the opportunities that would have emerged. The reach of the institution would have instantly expanded. When you take risks, you inevitably expand your reach beyond your comfort zone. Your reach is no longer local but can become global. You are not bound by your cultural or ethnic context. You are now reaching a more diverse market.

When you realign, nothing is off limits.

Don't try to be the best African American, Hispanic, or cultural system out there. **Be the best. Period.** When your system expands its reach, those connected to you have an expectation and an anticipation of it manifesting. Isaiah 54:2 (ESV) has always been my motivation for expanding the reach of my system, and it remains my prayer: "Enlarge the place of your tent, and let the curtains of your habitations be stretched out; do not hold back; lengthen your cords and strengthen your stakes."

REALIGN

Realignment is another important factor in making things work. Often the titles and positions that worked in one season of your organization are no longer relevant in another. You have to be able to realign staff to the needs of the people rather than realign people to the staff. This is why the people to whom you entrust your vision should have the capacity to grow with you and adapt in order that the system can remain vibrant, efficient, and effective.

When you realign, nothing is off limits. There may be programs or systems in place that need to be revamped. This may require an external evaluation, so that you are able to have a comprehensive understanding of what is working and what is not. Allowing others to examine your system gives you an unbiased opinion of the things that are needed within the system. You can't always see the real picture if you are in the frame.

One of the things we discovered during this process is that we had a lot of ministry that was functioning in name only but had not been active in some time. This required us to streamline in order to become more effective. We also had to reposition certain people in an effort to maximize their gifts while filling necessary gaps on the team. For example, rather than just have receptionists answer the phones, they are also administrative support to the team where there are gaps.

Realignment may be difficult for some on your team, because they have held certain positions for years. But, remember, you have to be willing to do what is necessary for the preservation of your vision. You cannot allow people to hold on to positions at the expense of the system.

You can't see the real picture if you are in the frame.

One of the things I've done over the years is study trends. When you make adjustments to your system, you have to do so with best practices in mind. Your decisions cannot be based on what is currently happening around you but what is coming down the road. So often we make decisions, and then we find out that once they are executed they are already outdated. When you have a variety of people engaging your system at all times, it's important that what you implement is cutting-edge and futuristic. This is why great leaders think outside the box.

MAKING IT WORK REQUIRES WORK

You've got to roll up your sleeves and be willing not only to see the big picture but pay attention to the details. You cannot expect what you do not inspect. This is not a call to micromanagement. Rather, it is a plea to revisit the distance between you and those you trust with your vision.

As your systems begins to grow, don't lose sight of what is important. The people who engage your system have to be the priority. They are the ones who support the vision you have and who experience the greatest impact from what it produces. Remain *people-oriented*, and it will heighten your sensitivities to their needs and concerns. Always keep the lines of communication open, so that you can be aware of what's occurring at the ground level within the system. Put safeguards in place to prevent gaps from frequently occurring. The system is the engine that drives the vision; and like every engine, you have to allow for servicing and checkups.

When people see your heart, they will trust your hand.

Work demands *follow-through*. This is important because the reason a lot of systems fail is because people within the system don't make *follow-through* a priority. If you are consistently hearing "Nobody got back with me," it must be addressed.

Everybody working in the system must be committed to *follow-up* and creating a culture of customer care that assures people that their needs are a priority. When *follow-through* does not occur, it sends a message that the person is not valued within the system. Every person must be viewed as valuable, and every inquiry must be addressed. It may be helpful to implement a 24- or 48-hour return call or email policy that can assure excellence in your system.

We live in a fast-paced world, and before people wait on you to get back to them, they will move on to other options to get what they need. Your response time is critical to the success of your system. Success is in the follow-through, tying up loose ends and treating each person as a valued child of God.

CREATING A POSITIVE EXPERIENCE

Executing vision requires that you effectively manage your system. Inputs and outputs provide ways for you to measure the system's effectiveness, which can be useful as you make adjustments moving forward. The goal is creating a positive experience for those who engage the system. When people see your heart, they will trust your hand.

The vision you have touches real people. Don't lose sight of that. Make certain that your vision does not get convoluted in a complex system and execution never takes place. Policies, procedures, and protocols are important, but they should never take precedence over people.

Creating a positive experience means that you put people first. Our mantra is, Relationship over rules. This means that we cannot allow a rule to ruin a relationship. If that were the case, the woman Jesus met at the well would have never experienced His power and presence. The woman with the issue of blood would still be sick. The ten lepers would still be on the side of the road.

Jesus put relationships over rules, not to get people to like him but so that those who encountered Him would experience transformation. It was for their sake, not His. This is our commitment:

Those who we encounter will have a positive experience. They will know they are loved as children of God, and they will leave having experienced the love of God.

SYSTEM MAINTENANCE

Fixing and maintaining systems is an ongoing project. Don't allow set-backs or failures to discourage you. Robert Green, the author of the book *Mastery*, provides the following perspective on failure:

> There are two kinds of failure. The first comes from never trying out your ideas because you are afraid, or because you are waiting for the perfect time. This kind of failure you can never learn from, and such timidity will destroy you. The second kind comes from a bold and venturesome spirit. If you fail in this way, the hit that you take to your reputation is greatly outweighed by what you learn. Repeated failure will toughen your spirit and show you with absolute clarity how things must be done.[1]

Your vision is too important give up. People are depending on what you have you to offer. It's often easy to look at "successful" people and think that it has all come easily to them. In many cases, this is not what happened.

- Thomas Edison tried almost 10,000 times before he succeeded in creating the electric light.
- The original business plan for what was to become Federal Express was given a failing grade on Fred Smith's college exam. And, in the early days, their employees would cash

1 Greene, R. (2012). *Mastery*. New York: Viking.

their paychecks at retail stores, rather than banks. This meant it would take longer for the money to clear, thereby giving Fed Ex more time to cover their payroll.

- Sylvester Stallone had been turned down a thousand times by agents and was down to his last $600 before he found a company that would produce his movie *Rocky*. The rest is history!
- The poet Robert Frost had his first poetry submissions to *The Atlantic Monthly* returned unwanted.
- Colonel Sanders went to more than 1,000 places trying to sell his chicken recipe before he found an interested buyer.
- Ray Kroc, the business man who turned McDonald's into a global franchise, knew this, too. "Nothing in this world can take the place of persistence," he once said. "Talent will not; nothing is more common than unsuccessful men with great talent. Genius will not. Un-rewarded genius is almost a proverb. Education will not. The world is full of educated derelicts. Persistence, determination alone are omnipotent."[2]

Remain determined to see your vision manifest to the fullest extent. Execute with character and resilience. There may be some missteps along the way, but your goal should be the preservation of vision and how it ultimately will touch the world in a positive way.

---

2 https://storiesforpreaching.com/category/sermonillustrations/perseverance/.

QUESTIONS

1. What is your system, and how does it operate?
2. How do you fix and maintain your system?
3. Have you ever had a "gatekeeper experience"? What happened?
4. Who are the people on your team? Does your team maximize each person's skills and talents, or are they squandering them? How can you help your team be more cohesive and effective?
5. How do you handle risk? What are the benefits of risk in light of your vision?

12

THE BALANCING ACT

One of the questions I'm often asked is how I balance it all. This is an area that has hindered many people from being productive and executing vision. I want to address balance from two perspectives. First, I want to deal with what it takes to multitask and effectively manage life alongside work. Second, I want to address how balance should manifest in our lives, which allows us to be well-rounded. Both of these areas are challenges but well within the reach of those who desire to achieve it. When we are balanced, our ability to produce increases and our vision is sustainable.

I. WORK-LIFE BALANCE

Balance Your Time

When our steps are ordered by God, our life is in order. One of the first areas where many people struggle to find balance is in their use of time. Time management is tough. It's a lifelong skill. The way you manage time gives insight into your personal discipline. Proverbs 16:9 says, "A man's heart plans his way: but the LORD directs his steps."

Time management includes the following elements:

1. *Create a Workable Schedule*

Creating a daily schedule can be completed by using simple strategies on paper or with the use of technology. A workable schedule includes planning daily, weekly, and monthly activities. Your workable schedule must be just that, a schedule that makes it possible to work. Your day-to-day activities must be realistic. Do not overcrowd your schedule with things you hope to do, but include things that can realistically be completed in the timeframe allotted. Purpose should determine your schedule. If it's not in your purpose, why is it on your schedule?

2. *Anticipate the Unexpected*

When creating a workable schedule, delays must be considered so you will not be late or fall behind schedule. Unavoidable traffic delays such as accidents, detours, and inclement weather should be considered when attempting to make scheduled appointments. By building extra time in your schedule, you will avoid being late and will remain in control of your time.

3. *Be in Control of Your Time*

Effective time management is recognizing that you are in control. Being in control of your time by being on time is an indicator that your time and the time of others is priority in your life. Time should never have control over you; you should always be in control of your time. Ephesians 5:16 says, "Redeeming the time, because the days are evil." You have to avoid the time-snatchers.

> The steps of a good man are ordered by the LORD: and he delights in his way.
> —Psalm 37:23

There are four things that rob people of precious productive time.

- **Addictions.** Addictions occupy much of our time, because we are consumed and drawn to them. The need to feed our addictions causes us to compromise time allocated for more productive assignments.
- **Unhealthy relationships.** When we are in unhealthy relationships, we often spend unnecessary time attempting to accommodate them. Unhealthy relationships compete for productive time slots, whereas healthy relationships compliment them. All the time spent trying to normalize what otherwise would be abnormal is costly.
- **Too many responsibilities.** Some people just don't know how to say no. As I said earlier, no is an answer. When you continue to take on responsibilities, it robs you of the time needed to accomplish the things you need to do. You can't complain

about time getting away from you if you keep offering it up to every invitation that presents itself.

- **Social media.** Social media is a powerful tool if used effectively. But whenever you check your timeline every ten minutes or post every 20 minutes, you can be lulled away from your work and look up and hours have passed you by.

4. *Commit to Being Punctual*

Being punctual is an indicator that you value time, and it also means you value the time of others. When we are late, it sends the message that another person's time is not valuable. Be considerate, be professional, and be on time. I've learned that there are ways to develop greater balance in this area.

Set Goals

Goals should always be SMART (Specific, Measurable, Attainable, and Relevant).

Specific and measurable mean that you are sure you know what you want to achieve and when.

Attainable and relevant mean to make sure you genuinely want to achieve the goal; make sure it is not the goal of someone else or a personal goal of time past and is no longer relevant.

Set Priorities and Meet Them

After goals are set, the method of achieving the goals must be established. Prioritizing the goals will help in knowing how to manage time as it relates to the goal, and it helps with not feeling overwhelmed with a specific task.

Overcome Procrastination

Procrastination is a major cause of waste and failure. *Procrastination* is defined as "to defer action, delay, to procrastinate until an opportunity is lost." There is a common mindset that robs people of so many possible accomplishments. This mindset is often seen in religious matters, defeating Christians and paralyzing local churches. But procrastination is not new. There are plenty of examples in the Bible.

Luke 14:15-24 is a parable of God's invitation to people to partake of His blessings. However, the parable shows that many will be at God's feast. Some will defer because they have "bought a piece of ground" (Luke 14:18). Another said, "I have bought five yoke of oxen, and I am going to test them" (Luke 14:19). A third said, "I have married a wife, and therefore I cannot come" (Luke 14:20). They each deferred action and missed out on a wonderful opportunity because they procrastinated.

> To everything there is a season, and a time for every purpose under heaven.
>
> —Ecclesiastes 3:1

In Acts 26, King Agrippa says, "Almost thou persuaded me to be a Christian" (Acts 26:28, KJV). Agrippa was almost persuaded, but he did not act on what he had heard. Often, we are in the same predicament as King Agrippa, having heard a compelling word, which led to conviction, but we did not convert because of the comfort and convenience of our current situation. Your delay can lead to your destruction.

If you are going to execute vision, overcome the debilitating effects of procrastination. But before there can be any meaningful undertaking, there must be introspection. Take an honest look at yourself. One way to avoid wasteful procrastination is by having the right value system. As seen in the parable of the Great Supper, each person had his own priorities that kept him from accepting the invitation. "I do not have time to serve God" simply means people put other priorities ahead of God. We must first seek matters pertaining to God (Matthew 6:33).

It is possible to lie to ourselves. For instance, I might say, "I shall, Lord willing, go by tomorrow and check on Sister So-and-So and see how she's doing." The next day arrives and I say, "I know I meant to check on Sister So-and-So, but I have to watch a movie that I just discovered is coming on during the time I had allotted to visit her." Be honest with what you intend to do. Set a time, and do it. Even better than a mental list is a physical list, and an office calendar is also invaluable in implementing needed tasks.

Successful people in the Bible were always people of immediacy. They did not defer (Acts 10:33; 16:33). It has been said that tomorrow is the busiest day of people's lives, because many people defer until tomorrow what they should do today. Hence, they never address and perform these tasks. If you are going to have balance, put things in proper order based on priorities. There are some things you actually have to do and some you don't.

Here are some steps to overcoming procrastination.

- Acknowledge the consequences of failure to be on time or have work submitted on time; then get started.
- Create a to-do list. This helps with staying on task and prevents falling behind.

- Break big jobs down into smaller steps. Target the easy-to-accomplish tasks first.
- Celebrate small wins. Reward yourself for completing tasks on schedule.

Work-life balance is a key component for a successful life. Having healthy work-life balance is essential to getting your life in order. Gaining and maintaining balance puts you on a path toward living a rewarding life. When you are serious about balancing all the things in your life, be intentional about giving everything a place. Organize your life so that you are able to execute effectively and efficiently.

I oversee a lot of things at the same time. I sit on two university boards, one of which I chair. I sit on a bank board, lead a church of over 30,000 members, alongside leading a reformation of two million people around the world. I am also a husband and a father. You can imagine what my schedule looks like. I have discovered that when you create work-life balance you can accomplish anything you set out to do without being stressed.

Much of my life is lived on a schedule. I place significant boundaries around my family time so there is no encroachment from work-related areas. When I'm on, I'm on. When I'm off, I'm off. You do what you have to do until you can do what you want to do. Balance requires you to be able to produce at a high level in every area of your life while maintaining the order and structure along the way. First Corinthians 14:40 says, "Let all things be done decently and in order."

II. PERSONAL BALANCE

Once you have developed work-life balance, develop balance in your personal life. This is an area I'm passionate about, because I believe the work we do should not cost us our health or our families. As you execute vision, it is important that you are able to exemplify balance in four critical areas: faith, family, fitness, and finance. When I became presiding bishop of the Full Gospel Baptist Church Fellowship, these four areas became the focus of my vision. I have seen incredibly gifted people who functioned well in their assignments, but other areas of their lives were getting a failing grade. If you are able to execute vision and have balance in these areas, you will achieve success.

God will take you where you are willing to take Him.

Faith

In this fast-paced world, it is important that we don't lose sight of our faith. Balance requires that our relationships with God remain central. God will not take you where you are not willing to take Him. Never get too busy that you don't pray. If you are too busy to pray, you are too busy. If you are too busy to read His word, you are too busy. Keeping your faith in perspective helps to put life in perspective. If you tell God you're too busy to spend time with him in worship, prayer, or devotion, He might just free you up from the job so you can no longer complain.

Family

Family balance is huge. I've seen many people sacrifice their marriages and families on the altars of trying to be successful. It means nothing for me to minister to thousands in my church and reach millions around the world if my children never have access to my wife and me. Family balance means you've got to make sure you keep certain times sacred so that you can pour into your family. God will never give you a vision that will put a strain on your family. Properly executing vision suggests that you build your schedule around your family first.

My wife and I set our calendar first, and then everything else is scheduled around it. When we schedule a vacation, those times are nonnegotiable. Once, I left an important meeting with my suit and dress shoes on to take my daughter to the pumpkin patch, because I had decided that this outing with my daughter was a priority. Although the meeting was important, I left early so I could pick up my daughter from school. To see the expression on her face was priceless. There I was, standing in the pumpkin patch with dress shoes on and enjoying this moment with my daughter.

The meeting went on without me, and it was successful. My daughter knew nothing of the matters of the meeting. All she knew was that her daddy took her to the pumpkin patch. Don't get so busy that you miss your "pumpkin patch" experiences. You won't get a chance to get those moments back. At the core of this experience was the fact that my daughter believes her daddy keeps his word.

Fitness

When I use the word *fitness*, I am talking about more than just working out; I'm talking about holistic health. This is one of the areas that many people take for granted. I know many gifted people who have died too soon from preventable diseases, and the church is often guilty of helping people dig their graves with their forks. We glorify *late-night* eating after service. We prepare fried foods and dishes full of sugar while contributing to the high rates of diabetes, heart disease, and obesity. This also happens in the business world. Too many people work late hours on stressful jobs while eating poorly.

If we are going to be balanced, we have to take our health seriously. Have you ever considered that Jesus endured Roman persecution and yet had the strength to carry the cross to Calvary? There is no way He could have fulfilled His assignment had He not been in good physical condition. The same applies to us. It is imperative that we take our health seriously, so that we are able to walk out our assignment with the stamina it requires.

It saddens me to see incredibly gifted people who neglect this area. You can't blame the devil for attacking your health if you are a co-conspirator in the things you put into your body. Third John 2 (KJV) says, "Beloved, I wish above all things that you mayest prosper and be in health, even as your soul prospereth."

Your success means nothing if you are not healthy enough to enjoy it. God is not interested in opening new opportunities for you if you are not interested in taking care of yourself. How can you ask God to enlarge your territory, if you don't have the strength to get to it? A balanced life demands great attention be given to your health. Poor health produces poor execution.

Finances

The final area of balance is finances. This area is important because God is interested in funding purpose. We must be good stewards of the resources we have so that we are able to leave a legacy. I share with the people who work on our team that it is not God's will for you to work all your life and have nothing to show for it. Making wise financial decisions is essential. Open your hands before you, and look at them. How much money has passed through those hands that you wish you could get back? I know that is a painful exercise for some, but it should challenge us all to start making intelligent financial decisions.

There are a lot of great projects that never get off the ground because of a lack of funds. In many cases, there are legitimate reasons the funding is not there, but for some it's the result of poor financial planning. When you execute vision, you must think legacy. Think about creating an endowment, so the vision will extend several generations after you.

> For where your treasure is, there your heart will be also.
>
> —Matthew 6:21, KJV

Create a culture about money so that those who inherit your vision don't squander it. How many businesses have you seen passed on to children who didn't know how to manage money and the businesses closed? In some cases, visions that have been impacting lives for over 50 years can be destroyed in less than one year because there is no financial responsibility. I share with people in the church that God doesn't mind us giving Him glory and shouting, but when we get through, we should be able to pay our bills. The reason many of our businesses, churches, and personal finances are in trouble is because there is no balance in this area.

Finances also mean being generous by giving to God and those in need. Just as God blessed Abraham to be a blessing, He also blessed you for the same reason. Don't hoard your money. Be discerning and wise, but remember that God generously shared Jesus with us. Be generous with others.

CONCLUSION

No Opportunity Wasted is about putting your love of God into practice, so you can be successful, *family-focused*, healthy, and financially stable at the same time. You don't have to settle for one or two and live without the others. I believe that your purpose is lived out better when your life is balanced. As you execute vision, remember that it requires you to perform at optimal capacity. When you do that, you are ready to seize every opportunity that is in alignment with your purpose, and you can consistently live a life producing results. Don't waste your moment!

QUESTIONS

1. Where do you struggle in trying to find balance? Why? How can you create more balance in your life?
2. List the things that are important to you, in order of importance. What's at the top of the list? What's at the bottom? Do you think God is pleased with your list? How could you change your list to better glorify God and, at the same time, find balance?
3. How does your faith inform what you prioritize on a daily, weekly, monthly, or yearly basis?
4. Evaluate your finances. Do they line up with your vision?
5. Have you created checkpoints along your journey that keep you in line with your vision?

CPSIA information can be obtained
at www.ICGtesting.com
Printed in the USA
BVHW070051281221
624776BV00011B/685/J

9 780997 431858